The End Times
(New information for personal peace)

Channelled Teachings
Given in Love

Kryon
Book I

What the readers are saying...

"...Every page has spoken directly to my heart and has most certainly been a powerful contributor in awakening the Christ within."
DH – "Fountain of Life Institute" – Hawaii

"...My excitement rose as I read each page such that I have thought of nothing else since I began."
RIG – Canada

"...We love this book Kryon "The End Times"! We feel extremely exited and thrilled with it! Seems more like in reality, our 'beginning times' ... awesomely wonderful. Thank you very much!"
PB – "Reevis Mountain school of Self-Reliance" – Arizona

"...I'm so impressed with the material - Thank you for putting it into a book! It feels to me as if Kryon's information is, literally, saving my life, and I am so grateful to you for your willingness to receive and publish this information."
CF – New Mexico

"Enclosed is a check for the book. I don't even know what the book is about, but two good friends phoned me, one from San Francisco and one from Washington D.C., to tell me I had to get it and read it, so here goes..."
MB – Iowa City, IA

What the readers are saying...

"...I read the book, and it REALLY RESONATED with my being! It seemed:

       *accurate channeling,
       *true information,
       *timely information very relevant to
what's happening now on the planet.

I was so moved by your book, that I intend to get a few copies to give to my friends. It was a book that I just did not want to put down."

Iasos
Composer, arranger, international recording artist
1990 *Crystal Award* recipient - International New Age Music Conference
Inter-Dimensional Music
Sausalito, CA

"The clarity of the message and the experience of loving energy gleaned from Kryon is the distilled essence which has stayed with me since reading the book. It is needed, clear and straight forward."

Christina Thomas
Director of Inner Light Institute
Author of *Secrets* and *In Tune With The Soul*
Tennessee

To Jan...
for the patience...

The End Times
New information for personal peace
Kryon Book 1

Publisher:

The Kryon Writings

1155 Camino Del Mar – #422
Del Mar, California 92014
[www.kryonqtly.com]

Books can be purchased in retail stores,
or by phone - Credit cards welcome.
(800) 352-6657

Author: Lee Carroll

Copyright © 1993 by Lee Carroll
First paperback printing - November 1993
Second paperback printing - May 1994 - Revised
Third paperback printing - October 1994
Fourth paperback printing - January 1995
Fifth paperback printing - April 1995
Sixth paperback printing - Aug 1995
Seventh paperback printing - Dec 1995
Eighth paperback printing - Mar 1996
Ninth paperback printing - August 1996
Tenth paperback printing - April 1997 - Revised
Eleventh paperback printing - March 1998
Twelfth paperback printing - July 1998
Thirteenth papeback printing - January 1999

Printed in the United States of America

ISBN# 0-9636304-2-3 : $12.00 Paperback U.S.A.

c

Table of Contents

Foreword...

When planet earth reaches a time of dimensional shift and change, it is important to remember that the Universe (which we know as God) never abandons us. One of the ways source shares its love is to provide information from knowledgeable intelligences by having teachers born into body. Another way this is done is by having teachers trance through a loving channel who can be trusted not to misrepresent, alter or misuse this needed support. The tranced information then assists us in understanding and in making personal adjustments with grace and ease.

The messages from Kryon in these "changing times" is intellectually stimulating and spoken beautifully with unconditional love. I personally know and respect both Lee Carroll and Kryon. Lee is a faithful and dedicated channel of Kryon's words. As one who has worked and taught in the field of Metaphysics for twenty-five years, I find the information clear and thought provoking. The knowledge brought through is most pertinent to our changing world. You will find yourself filled with the love energy of Kryon. I am using the text of Kryon's words as recommended reading for my students and as a tool for thought in the classes I teach. And so it is with great enthusiasm that I await further information from Kryon and further publication by Lee Carroll.

Barbra Dillenger, MscD

Chapter One

Meet Kryon

Kryon Channelling

The writings begin...

From the writer...

These next few pages may contain some of the most enlightening glimpses yet as to the way things work from the entity known to me as "Kryon." As the Channelling/writer, I have had the extraordinary privilege of putting Kryon's messages on paper. I have known of Kryon for some time, and have essentially ignored him. It took two psychic readers unknown to each other, three years apart, to actually spell his name out loud in a session and say that he was of importance and so... sheepishly I plopped myself down at the word processor and began to transcribe Kryon's messages to all of us.

Immediately, Kryon gave us a very loving look at a prime issue: The subject of Jesus Christ, who he really is, and a good synopsis of the Metaphysical belief system (Chapter 6 in this book). Kryon even gave us new interpretations of the Holy Scripture... and I almost didn't write it down, I was so startled by the boldness! (I was also afraid lightning might strike me at any moment, an obvious cultural influence). Kryon is speaking directly to humans in the western world through these writings, and he seems to relate to what is happening to us personally right now.

I am told repeatedly to be still and write, and not to complain about what I get... and not to worry about what others may say (Kryon is very practical and very direct). He reminds me constantly that I am under contract to do this, and that we have had service together in the past. Naturally I have no direct knowledge of what he is talking about, since I am very much a part of Earth, and very skeptical of just about everything until it hits me on the head enough times... as Kryon has. Believe me, this experience is highly unusual for me. I am a businessman who hasn't channelled anything more than my TV set for 48 years... and now this! There is something urgent, serious, and at the same time very loving, from this high entity beyond the veil (as Kryon calls it).

This writing is for the more Metaphysical of you. Kryon wants to speak about the other side of the veil, and who he is, why he is here, and a little of what is coming up for us on Earth. He doesn't like to be genderized (as I have done in this sentence), but I refuse to call the entity an "it," and calling him a "shim" (she/him) contraction won't do either. So I revert to a him whenever I absolutely have to for syntax. Kryon has one recurring theme, and I am given the repeated message that it is very important: "LOVE is the most powerful force in the entire Universe. It is the glue that will bond our belief together, instead of the doctrine that does it for the other systems. Love is not being recognized for its power, and it is not being used by us correctly." I think that as these writings proceed, further chapters will expound on what we should do to solve this.

If you have no knowledge of the Metaphysical belief system, I suggest you read more about it within the sixth chapter of this book (Jesus Christ – who he really was); otherwise what follows may sound very strange indeed! Those of you with some knowledge of the Universal belief system will be more at home with what is to come.

Kryon wants me to write for the common person, not the one who has been part of the "new age" movement for years and years. He admonished me very early on to keep the process simple and direct, and has given me good methods in which to do so. Those who have been in the movement for many years won't have any problems with this kind of writing, but Kryon tells me that there may be some resistance from the old timers due to new interpretations. It seems that we are entering a time where information is going to be much clearer. In the past a great deal of information had the right thrust, but the wrong facts, and now we are going to clear some of this up.

This book features the first time that Kryon will come forward and speak in the first person. Within the entire book I am actually typing as it comes, with very little steering correction along the way. I have been very clearly instructed to do this, and to let the grammar fall where it may and the communication flow... the result is a style that is a bit ragged, but you will read it with the same 'first time' spontaneity that it was written.

What follows, therefore, we will both see for the first time... myself as the writer and you as the reader. Most chapters will have writer's notes before them, and each time there will be comments written before the actual Kryon communication.

...And now, meet Kryon.

Meet Kryon
Chapter One

Who am I?

Greetings! I am Kryon, of magnetic service. Each one of you is loved dearly! If you have been brought to a point where you are reading this communication, you are in the right place at the right time. Please continue. I am speaking directly to you.

I speak to you now as clearly as I can through my partner; but I cannot use language as you know it, so the actual words are still being translated through his mind. My communications are actually independent of any language. I speak to you in "thought packages" and "idea groups," translated into your words so that you can understand.

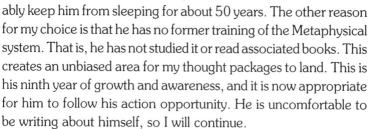

I have chosen this writer for several reasons, the main one being that he agreed to do this before he came in. He has a contract, but as any human he can choose not to do this if he wants. He also intuitively knows that if he doesn't do this, I will probably keep him from sleeping for about 50 years. The other reason for my choice is that he has no former training of the Metaphysical system. That is, he has not studied it or read associated books. This creates an unbiased area for my thought packages to land. This is his ninth year of growth and awareness, and it is now appropriate for him to follow his action opportunity. He is uncomfortable to be writing about himself, so I will continue.

My name isn't really Kryon, and I am not a man. I wish I could impart to you what it is like to be the entity that I am, but there are basic human implants of psychological restriction that simply will not let you understand. I will expound on this later. My *name* is a "thought group" or "energy package" that surrounds me and is recognizable by all other entities. This same package is sent in my communications and identifies me at all times. I am constantly in communications with all – please simply accept this. The spelling of my name I gave to those who needed it came in a thought package and is as close to my TONE sound as I could get for your language. There is really much more to my name than the sound, and I would really like you to be able to "feel" it; but you are unable at this time.

My name energy package (which is different than my communications energy package) consists of three parts: (1) TONE – What you perceive as sound, but is perceived here in a non auditory fashion, (2) LIGHT FREQUENCY – what you perceive as light and color, and (3) FORM – what you perceive as shapes and designs. It is presented singularly as one package, and perceived in a way which is not significant to you at this time. Most of my name package is out of the range of any of your human senses.

This is very difficult to explain. It would be like explaining your colors to a sightless human. You have not been given the receptors that will give the understanding as to how I am perceived, and this is as it should be.

It is very interesting to me that those humans "in touch" with this side of the veil for many years have not really put this energy package together yet. Your restrictive implant design is responsible for your two-dimensional reasoning, but those with balance should have been able to put this together before now. It's time to begin! You have many enlightened writings about the meanings of color, light, sound and shape design... and you recognize their significance. But you must think three dimensionally about these things, and put them together for them to be truly meaningful. To many these items separately just seem as loose knowledge, and are passively interesting. When you put them together and start to work with them, they will become alive with energy. Believe it! It is how things work.

What am I?

I am of magnetic service. This means two things to you, and I will start with the latter: service. My entity is one of service. I have never been a human or anything else but Kryon. My entire purpose is to serve in a specified capacity the "schools" throughout the universe where the entities such as yourselves are located. There are many schools of various levels, some that are lower and some higher than your own.

There are many kinds of entities, but the number is always the same. We are constant, and reflect the whole at all times. You are a very important part of the whole, and you are very special. You have elected to be the ones to bring the frequency of the whole to a higher level. This process is very interesting, and requires sacrifice and work. When you are on my side of the veil, there are many things which become logical and clear that make no sense whatsoever to you now. But the process of living, dying, working and experiencing the lessons of humanity is a staple to the final goal of our entire existence, and your process at this time is the most exciting of all. I will explain this as I continue.

Those such as myself who are in service have elected to work for the rest of you. There are many more of us in service than those of you in lesson, and there are many, many kinds of service. There are entities directly assigned to each of you. These entities move on as you reach different levels. Some never move on, and you have them for life. All of them are assigned for service to you directly.

To make things really complex for you, but quite logical and simple from my point of view, is the fact that your planet is the home for several kinds of schools simultaneous to your own that you are totally unaware of. That is, there are other entities that interact with you in an odd way which becomes their own school! You are their test! Some of the other biology you observe on Earth are really entities also, but you think of them as lower intelligence. Also there are ethereal entities that are with you that are working their way through lessons, and you perceive them as ghosts or apparitions, not to be confused with the apparitions that are assigned to you for service.

All of us in service celebrate you and your work. Many of you started in service, and elected to change. Some of you were invited to change, and did so willingly. The decisions of the whole always match the will of the individual. Love is the power source and it is of singular origin.

We are all linked together. We are the great "I AM" as your scriptures call God. When I send the message "**I am** Kryon," there is a communication that I belong to the whole, and my signature is **Kryon**. We are God. You are a piece of God, and you have the power to become as high on your side of the veil as you were before you came... and you are loved without measure. You are each high entities of your own who have agreed to be exactly where you are before you ever got where you are. We are all collective in spirit, even while you are on Earth, veiled from truth. Although we are collective, LOVE is singular and is of one origin, or focus. This may seem confusing, but consider it a fact that is of primary importance, so that you understand that it is special for your current time.

Who are You?

Before I continue to speak about my work for you, I must stop to try to explain why some of you are not believing anything you are reading right now. Formerly in another communication I spoke about an analogy where you as humans try to explain the workings of a complex piece of equipment to an Earth animal. This is very similar to me trying to explain anything of what is happening over on this side, to you on the other. This is as it should be, and is proper. In fact, a great deal of work has gone into making it so! Your power of intuition and discernment are the only things which will give you the choice to stop reading this or not, because everything else you own biologically has been tampered with! As I spoke of earlier, you have implants that will never let you understand this side of the veil on a reasoning level. There is only one way you can begin to understand, and it must be done by balancing your biology with your spirituality. You see, your spiritual side is pure and unaffected, and is still intact without restriction. With a balance of the power of your spiritual side, your biological (biological mind and physical body) structure will no longer be limited in scope of understanding. Many of you are calling this balance "enlightenment."

I want to give you an example of your limitations, but this is not to make you feel inferior (because you are not!). It is as an exercise in reason and logic to apply to what I am telling you. Each human is implanted with many limitations and restraints of conscious thought. For instance, you are all implanted with the feeling that everything must have a start and an end, a beginning and completion. If I told you that something always "was," you would have a difficult time with that. If I told you something always "was," and always "will be," you might say you under-stand... but you can't. You are implanted with this restriction, and you conceive everything as having a start. I cannot suddenly give you a bypass to this restriction, but I can cause you to question your perception by asking you to consider the following: Imagine you are now standing inside a large bubble. Can you show me where the bubble starts and ends? ... or perhaps how it originated? How can the interior of a sphere have a beginning? It's three dimensional! If you now take a pen and draw a line all around the inside of the bubble, you are showing yourself my lesson. You are creating for yourself a beginning and an end point (where you start your line and where you end it) in an environment that had none to begin with. You are actually superimposing your limitations on something that has none. <u>This is what has been done for you.</u> You have been biased to be two-dimensional in a three dimensional space, and all your thinking reflects this. You are also driven to constantly look for creation... which is your implant at work.

This is also related to the other basic restriction you are given: You perceive time as linear and constant, with only two dimensions, forward and back. Because it never pauses, you can never be in the "now." It is only in the last few generations that you have realized that time is relative (is not actually constant), but you still have no concept of its third dimension. If I told you that time as you know it doesn't exist at all, you would probably laugh out loud... Well, start laughing. The whole concept as you understand it was created for you to allow for your lessons, and to give you a linear, consistent platform on which to exist while you learn. Constant "reliable" time is an Earth concept. On the side where I am there is a very different kind of time, and everything is in the "now." Its third dimension is vertical. As in the bubble, there is no past or future, only now. Everything reflects to a center point, exactly where you are in the bubble.

With all of your scientific endeavors, you have been restricted to two dimensional thinking. You have not yet discovered the balance I spoke of, and have not related it to science. The spiritual sciences of the universe are logical, predictable, and are based on numbers and formulas that always work. It is a marriage of the physical and the spiritual, and proper implementation brings about consistent, observable changes. This is my service, and I know of these things. What you are missing is the balance with the spiritual part that will enable your science to leap forward in a spectacular manner when you achieve this balance.

As humanity proceeds in the next few years, you will be given the opportunity to see the results of the marriage of the physical, mental, and spiritual to achieve <u>real science</u>. You currently do not have real science, only two dimensional science... human science, not universal science.

The missing part, being the spiritual, has been shunned by your scientists all these hundreds of years as non-scientific. This is ironic in that the spiritual is where the real power and understanding is! You will never achieve sustained space travel without it. You will also never be able to alter or understand gravity, and most important, the transmutation of matter will never be yours without it. Imagine... how would you like to neutralize all your atomic waste, so that a child could play with it, as sand. It's not difficult to do, but it requires skills that you have not yet used, but that you now have the power and permission to develop. You have earned these things!

From my standpoint the power you have never used yet is in my domain. You have absolutely enormous raw power resources that exist through the understanding and regulated use of the magnetic fields of your planet. All the energy you ever need is there, not to mention the secret of passive flight using the magnetic grids. But you will not be able to understand it without balanced three dimensional science.

At this point humans are as tiny molecules on a giant magnet, a magnet which is able to move things with enormous force if called on, but humans are only able to see far enough to dig tiny holes in the surface and suck out minuscule pieces of iron to burn for heat and power. You are like ants on a generator, wishing for electricity. The forest has eluded you, while you concentrate on consuming one leaf for fuel!

Have you noticed the recurring theme of the **power of three**? There is no "magic" here as you call it, just universal logic. The number three vibration emanates power and energy. Balance of the "three" is necessary for you to proceed with enlightenment (physical, mental and spiritual). Knowledge in science of the three is necessary for you to use the real power at your disposal, and unlock the remaining scientific secrets left to you. Three also transmutes to "one" when used. This is difficult to explain, but consider mixing three dormant parts to create one active one, and you will understand it better. Much of your western religion is based around the three God parts combined into one Godhead. This information is a bit modified from its true meaning, but still accurate in concept of the power of three combining to make the one.

I have also told you of the three parts to my name. Together they communicate my "signature," and apart they are meaningless. Three is very important, and is constant throughout the universe.

Also of mild interest: if you take the letters of my TONE name KRYON, and assign a western alphabet number to each of the letters – A=1 B=2 Z=26 etc., then add up the numbers, you will result in the number 83, which then adds to create **11**. This is significant, and describes who I am even better to those of you who have intuitive knowledge of number meanings. This is why I chose the spelling in your language. *The spelling of my name was not supplied by your writer.* This number **11** will tell you of my character. When you multiply this number by the power vibration 3, it results in **33**, and will give you insight as to my SERVICE. I will give you an important power formula: **9944**. Your discernment and intuition will eventually lead you to the meaning of this, but it is important in the transmutation of energy.

My service to you is not to train you in these things. I spoke of the fact that I am of magnetic service. Others are here in service to help you with the procedures of balance, and the details you will need. All of us are here in love.

Why am I here?

Before I can tell you exactly why I am here, I must explain more about the way things work for you. You will then understand more about my service, and why I am here.

Many of you are reading this now with the hopes of gleaning something precious, perhaps something meaningful– something that comes from a longing in your soul to know the truth about things. This is your freshly awakened sense of spirituality: You recognize that there is something more to life than simply feeding yourself and protecting yourself from perishing (another implant). Perhaps you have always felt there was something more, but had no idea what it could be. You are experiencing a gradual change of consciousness, which you have earned, and it is appropriate for your time. Continue your search. It will lead to what you really are longing for: peace of mind through the power of Love.

Humans have always searched for God. This is simply a home-sickness that reflects the absence of your connection to communication while you are in lesson. It is a basic cellular desire, and is global.

Things are beginning to change, and that's why I'm here. The old Earth, middle Earth, and new Earth refer to three basic consciousness levels of humans (not to be confused with time dispensations of human making) over the earthly time since the beginnings of the "in lesson" entities on Earth. We are now coming to the fourth level, which has tremendous potential and will be the last. It is the age of responsibility, or enlightenment. It is where you finally take charge.

There is one reason for all of your existence on Earth: You are in lesson for the purpose of raising the vibration of the whole. This is the overall reason, and is not fully explainable to you at this time. Your endeavors while in lesson create energy through your incarnations and subsequent elevation of the Earth consciousness. This energy is valuable to the whole, and transmutes negativity. Negativity is the "absence of enlightenment," and if left unchecked, will be found more and more unless we have those of you throughout the universe constantly in lesson. You therefore are instrumental in changing something very large and complex. Please accept this. There isn't much more you will be given about this while you are on Earth. This is not planetary information, but universal information.

Closer to home, on a planetary level, your challenge was to start without any enlightenment at all, and gradually work through multiple lessons and incarnations to a fully enlightened state. You are on the path so far, and are quickly approaching the end of the whole cycle. Again, your endeavors though this process actually create energy for the rest of us.

Most important, as humans you are to live through many experiences during lifetimes of expression, creating the energy needed to bring the vibration of the planetary consciousness to its highest attainable level. While doing this, each century was supposed to also bring an overall shift of spiritual enlightenment... and so far it has. Twenty centuries ago, you in the "first world" earned the gift of the great master Jesus. This entity is also in service, and is known by all of us throughout the universe as one of the highest vibrations in service. The visit caused a great deal of spiritual activity on Earth, and has had repercussions ever since. My first message to my partner explained this, and also it explained Jesus' message with more clarity than I do here (*see the latter part of this book*).

Other parts of the Earth also received knowledge through other great masters in service during these times. Various cultures received the "truth" at various times as they were ready, but it was a global effort. The knowledge that they all imparted was about your power as spiritual beings, and your relationship to the universe. At that time, you were all invited to carry the full enlightened "piece of God" with you at all times, and start your final expressions as enlightened entities on Earth.

Centuries before that you were not even able to contain the full "charge" of your entity, and could not carry it around with you! Only part of it. Energy centers and temples contained the balance of your collective power. One of your long enduring transient cultures even carried the energy with them from place to place. The significance of the temples in very ancient Earth history were much higher than today, since they were indeed the spiritual power centers... and had physical manifestations to show it.

Currently, when you incarnate into the Earth plane each time, there is a brief rest where you meet and communicate with the whole, and plan for your next expression or lesson. Your plan is often determined directly by what happened during the last expression. You have called this karma. You form a contract, or plan on what will be learned and experienced as you begin the next expression. Quite often you incarnate only for a brief time, dying while a child, or being terminated early through illness or accident. This may seem cruel to you, or an illogical thing for you to agree to do, but it is appropriate and it is correct for the whole. The timing of when you again incarnate is determined by the lesson group around you, some still on Earth, and some not. Sometimes your incarnation is almost entirely for the expression of another, and is quick.

This would seem to indicate that there is some type of predestination at work. There is not. Believe it! This is much misunderstood.

All incarnations are as clean slates with a purpose overlay (karma) and various "doors" of action offered during the cycle (contract plan). The karma may or may not be satisfied. If it is not, then there will be another opportunity through another expression (incarnation). An individual may or may not open any of the doors of action offered by the contract; it is up to the individual, and where her or his growth is at the time. All of this interrelates to the other entities around your expression. As a planetary group you have gone through many of the correct doors. You have done this collectively on your side of the veil, and it has resulted in an elevation of the whole. Again, you are to be congratulated. I can attest that this is not always the case in the universe. You had several opportunities to fail, and came through it well.

About my work: **Magnetic fields are very significant to your biology! In addition, magnetic fields can (and do) affect your spiritual consciousness. The magnetic field of**

your planet is necessary for your biological health, and is fine tuned to fit within your spiritual scheme.

The magnetic field of your planet was carefully placed for your health – and your lessons. Look around you. What other planets do you find with magnetic fields? It is not a natural occurring force. It was placed purposefully and carefully. You have not been able to leave your planet far enough or long enough to realize this fact, but when you do, you must carry a field with you to continue sanity and health, and it must be correct. This is basic for humans. If you find another planet with a magnetic field, it is a prime suspect for biological life, or its arrival in the future, or a "marker" that there used to be life there. No matter what the actual biology of the life form, it will have to be polarized to have a spiritual significance. Note this: the farther that the magnetic field is aligned from the axis of the planetary spin, the more enlightened is the life form. This is just part of the process, and a signal to look for.

Electricity is all around you, and you already are beginning to notice the negative effects of artificially created magnetic fields on your health. All artificial magnetic fields should be shielded from your body. You have the technology for this and should protect yourself. Some of the diseases that are typical only to your affluent western society are a direct result of many artificial magnetic fields around you.

For years you have understood that the basic thought processes of your minds were electric (and therefore had magnetic properties). So also you understand that your entire biology, from nerves to muscles, are electro-chemical in their function. Every organ in your body is "balanced" magnetically (polarized) and is sensitive to outside fields. Troubles with brain, thyroid, heart, kidney and adrenals are suspects for magnetic disturbance. Psychics are "reading" your own personal magnetic field (you all have one). More accurately, they are perceiving the balance of your field. And your science doctors routinely attach wires to your body to record your electro-magnetic impulses.

Please understand that the best thing you can do for yourself is to shield yourself. Let the magnetic properties of the planet do the job for your health. Do not use artificial methods to try to create balance. Stay away from large static magnets, or electrically energized magnets. Very important: examine where you sleep, and remove magnetic devices from you by at least 3 meters. This could be electric clocks (plugged into your electric power), television sets, sound playback and recording devices, loudspeakers, heating devices, and fans. Never use an electric cover device for heating yourself. Do not use a heating device in a water-filled sleeping containment area. All equipment you use that has a motor should never be continuously next to you, and should be shielded. Make certain that your artificial power carriers and distribution devices are not running directly over or next to your sleeping quarters.

Something that should have been obvious to you was again shielded by your implants: Magnetism is the "couch" that human consciousness & biology has been sitting in for its entire existence. It is mathematical and it has been designed (it also interrelates to your implant system). If you had realized this, and given it credibility on your planet earlier, many of your diseases would now be understood and dormant. You must balance magnetically what you put in your bodies! How has this escaped you? Would you carry large magnets into a fine-tuned, polarized area? The immunity disease you are now fighting on Earth is magnetically controllable. Spend some time altering its magnetic properties and watch what happens. Re-polarize it and test its virility. You may be surprised.

With all this, are you then surprised when I inform you of the importance of the Earth's magnetic field on you?

I am Kryon of magnetic service. I have created the magnetic grid system of your planet. The creation of your grid system took eons of Earth time. It was balanced and re-balanced to match the physical vibrations of your evolving planet. During the time I was initially here, what you now perceive as positive and negative Earth polarity was altered many times. Your science can prove this; look for soil strata that will show multiple "flips" of north and south polarity of the Earth during its development. (The Earth did not flip; only the polarity). All of this took place before you were allowed to exist. Your writer assisted me and was of magnetic service at that time. His connection to me is part of the reason I am speaking through him now.

I have been here two other times since, for major global adjustment. This is my third adjustment, and my fourth and final visit. The last two times I was here, it was necessary and appropriate to make a global adjustment to accommodate your growth. In each case, humanity was terminated for this purpose. A few entities remained in each case to propagate the biology.

This may sound harsh to you, but it was correct and done in perfect harmony and love. All of you agreed to it beforehand, and it was a celebration, for it represented milestones in Earth growth! I am not here to tell you that my third adjustment will require your termination, but without some understanding many of you will terminate yourselves anyway. This third adjustment has already begun... and those of you who follow such things as the movement of magnetic north will know what I am talking about.

About The End Times

Many of you who are in touch with my side of the veil have foreseen what I am doing; but because the communication was difficult at best, you have not seen the correct plan. The information was correct, but the thought packages you received brought you to conclusions based on partial understanding that do not represent the actual facts. Your psychic visions were of some kind of tilting of the Earth. Nothing of this kind of thing is eminent. Even a very slight tilt of the Earth at this time would result in cataclysmic destruction of humanity. Oceans would spill onto landmasses, the Earth's crust would buckle violently, the moon would tug at newly exposed weaker areas and literally churn up the surface, and your weather would change dramatically. New active volcanoes would pop up everywhere, and humanity would end. How do I know this? I watched the process the first time! Certainly there will be floods and quakes and eruptions in your future... some will be a reaction to my new work, but these will not terminate the population. They will be in unusual places, however.

Use the discernment and intuition that is yours at your cellular level. Your higher consciousness "God self" will serve you for an answer: Do you think that humankind has been brought to the end of this cycle of higher consciousness enlightenment through entire Earth history to be snuffed by a wave or a boulder? Quite a graduation don't you think?

No. The tilt that has been foreseen is my job. It is a magnetic tilt, and will be the realignment of the grid system of the Earth to provide for your final time. Basically, you will be provided with a magnetically correct overlay for humans of balanced enlightenment to exist and live. Your magnetic north will no longer line up with polar north. It really never has that you know of, but its tilt will now become significant.

So why is this important? The importance is that those who are not ready will not be able to deal with it. Some will stay, and those who can't will reincarnate and re-emerge with the correct alignment. What this will do to your society is the negative part of my message.

My process will take ten to twelve Earth years to accomplish. From now through the year 2002 will be the gradual change. Around the year 1999 you should know exactly of what I am speaking. Governments are run by men of power... not all of them are enlightened. Their inability to deal with the consciousness alteration could imbalance them, and the result could be chaos.

You will note that I said "could be." This is where you get your real opportunity to make a change. As the grids adjust over the next years, you will be given more enlightenment. As I told you earlier, your restrictive implants are aligned to my grids. The grid alteration will free you of certain restrictions, and you will be able to control what you do from here to a degree that you never had before. For the first time you will be able to grasp completely the power that is available through the love energy, and use it for planetary healing. You will also be able to focus this energy in such a way that negative is transmuted to positive. This will result in the balance of many individuals that formerly would not have had a chance to remain during the transition.

Before I continue I am constantly being interrupted by the writer who wants to know about the significance of the triple six, or your 666 number that has been equated to the anti-God or anti-Christ end times. In addition, he wants to know about the "mark of the beast." The "mark" has been equated by humans to everything from your government's assigned work number to the computer code on the packages you purchase in the stores. Actually it is far more basic than that; it is the magnetic balance of your cellular biological code (DNA)! Therefore, all of you who are balanced are neutral. The ones who are not are "marked" for change (although this can be altered at any time). The "beast," as it has been called, is the unenlightened self in each of you. It was called the "beast" because of the potential actions of the unbalanced leaders during the upcoming realignment times... as the "beast" among you devouring the peace. Therefore, the unbalanced have the mark of the potential beast.

This may appear backwards to those of you who studied the channelled writings of the Christian book of Revelation... but now I have a revelation for you: This ancient channelling was purposely kept confusing and vague since **not one entity in the universe could ever predict the actual outcome of your on-coming test!** There are several possible endings for you, and this scripture book contains all the possible scenarios for Earth's end times presented at once. No wonder the interpretation is difficult... a "cosmic joke." The significance of the 666 is a phantom (or disguised) **9**. The number **9** is hiding in this triple six at every junction and represents the energy of your time now. It deals with a vibration of balance, power and love. It also signals completion. If you add the three 6 numbers, they equal 18, which adds to **9**. If you wish to multiply the resulting 9 by the power number 3 to obtain additional information about it (as you did with my name TONE earlier), you will receive 27, which also adds to **9**. If you feel the three 6's represent the number 6 times itself (or six cubed), you will obtain 216, which also adds to **9**. This 9 vibration is of those who will be balanced and remain. 666 is not the number to be feared. (There is no such thing as a number to be feared. Numbers give us important information, and are a wonderful three dimensional tool [only two dimensions of which you are now using]. They are mathematical, but they display energy.)

The significance of the three 6's together is as follows: Each 6 represents one of the three "math base six" calculations of the

Earth: (1) The first 6 is **time**. This base six system was derived from the Earth's rotation, and you have used it faithfully from its original discovery. (2) The second 6 represents the **magnetic compass system** of 360 degrees, developed again through the demands of Earth's physical properties, being circular. Note that the compass is also a "circle of 9's." Each of the eight 45-degree points add to nine. In addition the opposite headings of each of the eight added together also equal 9 (360+180; 45+225; 90+270; etc.). Why add the opposite headings? If you travel one direction for long enough, you will eventually find yourself standing in the place you left. Your path became one line that circled the globe. Its significance as a direction, therefore, must be considered by both its magnetic headings, since it now has no beginning or end. (3) The final base six system is **gravity**. When you are able to calculate it and manipulate it, you will discover it is also a base six system. The specter of a human entity representing the power of darkness on Earth who had an evil number on its head was not channelled information. It therefore was created by men for men's purposes. The "anti-Christ" notion came out of the fact that the unbalanced ones will carry the unenlightened energy which is contrary to the great love messages of the master Jesus.

Remember, you must move away from any previous ideas of what the "end times" should mean to you. If you are of the Christian faith, then I would ask you to please continue to keep your eyes on Jesus the teacher, and in perfect love ask for guidance – not based in men's doctrine, but in God's wisdom. Ask and pray for discernment and peace. Love will bring you through. There is great danger now for you. Men will bring you down if you are not careful. Claim the power of love that you are so familiar with, and use it! Ask for guidance from spirit (The Holy Spirit) about the true meaning of the end times, and what you should do. Study the "Jonestown incident" in your recent history, and learn from it.

The realignment that I am creating will certainly cause things to change for all of you. As I previously mentioned, it will cause the society of Earth to change through the actions of the governments involved in making the decisions for the masses. Those countries with self-balancing economies could be affected the most. It takes mutual, collective agreement and a more than marginal trust in the leadership of a government to allow for a self-balancing economy. When these factors are removed, collapse is certain. Those of you in the first world should be on alert for this. Balanced entities will come into their power in a strong way, but they should be circumspect with economical matters. Do not trust your government's monetary systems during this change. Change your personal monetary exchange medium to the most basic form. Barter for what you can, and do not put your faith in any monetary institutions. It is not necessary for you to escape your government system, or go into hiding, unless you feel that you are actually in danger of your existence. Ride out the changes, and continue to hold on to the honorable principles that are the fair answers to how humans must organize themselves for the benefit of the most, with tolerance and love for the less.

These are safeguard suggestions, and don't necessarily signal horrible survival times ahead, or a holocaust. There is good news too: I arrived in 1989 to start my work. Without any changes in place, you had already begun to change. This is a true sign that the timing was perfect, and that you were "on course." With my primary moves in place, you reacted globally in a positive way, complementing much of the new consciousness. You must know that we celebrate you for this! There is no greater sign of enlightenment on a global level than (1) the desire for tolerance ,(2) the desire for peace, and (3) the elimination of everything that gets in the way of number 1 and number 2.

Did you notice the power of **9** in the year of my arrival? The 666 with its hidden meaning foretold it. Anyone with discernment could have easily picked the beginning year of my final work with you, and many did.

You also saw a small global war take place, created solely and seemingly by an entity who was unbalanced. It was global in the sense that for the first time all nations were instantly involved, and communicating for a solution. The entity who caused the conflict is your example of exactly the kind of illogical reaction of an unenlightened (unbalanced) human to the new alignment. He was very sensitive to the changes made already, and reacted for everyone to see. This is the danger I speak of that you must correct. Notice how his action caused many, many humans to terminate their cycle. This is truly the "beast" at work, willingly devouring the peace. This is the "anti-Christ" energy I spoke of.

How can you personally stay on course? What should you do now? My next words to you are the most important of all.

The Love Connection:

LOVE IS POWER! Your word is inarticulate and poor for this concept. Other Earth languages at least have many kinds of words for this energy. Love is not a word, or just a feeling. It is a power source! It is energy. You can call on it, turn it off and on, store it up, send it out and focus it for many uses. It is always available and will never fail you. It is the promise of the universe! It is the common thread that runs things. It is time you started to see this... and I mean in the universal sense that it really is your time! You are at last being given permission to use and understand this power source, and you have earned it!

You may want to use the word "God-Source" instead of love to give you an understanding of the meaning of the power. We are collective, but the power source is singular. This means that we all share a common oneness that is the power. This is similar to electricity as you are familiar with it. Notice that the common element in your circuits is always the "ground." No matter what the purpose of the circuit, or the strength of the circuit, it always has one return, or commonality, a oneness within a multi-faceted system.

The love God-Source is the power you receive when you call upon God for anything. Any entity calling specifically, verbally or otherwise for the power of God receives this love God-Source. It is literal, and will respond appropriately. Appropriately means that it will respond within the universal correctness of the call. Enlightened, balanced individuals are especially good at calling up and focusing the love God-Source. They have always been as clear pathways through an otherwise murky and resistant veil. Most of these individuals have been religious leaders through the ages, who used love as their basis for life. Their honest love for the universe, and others around them, and their tolerance for other's process and karma, was the key to their balance. Actual knowledge of the "way things work" was (and still is) unimportant. Holy men in India, China, Syria, Israel or anywhere else, have the same connection to the power source as a Christian evangelist in a meeting in middle America.

Why do I tell you this? So you will understand that the source is singular! ... and is yours as never before. With my realignment, your spiritual side can soar! You will receive a feeling of perfect alignment, of finally coming home. This is your entity actually seeing itself for the first time for what it is: a piece of God. A piece with a name known by all, that can never be destroyed, and can never be added to or subtracted from. Can you imagine what you can do now?

Transmutation

You must call upon this love God-Source to heal and balance the planet. There will be <u>guaranteed results</u> when you do this. You must gather with others of like balance to focus your energies for this. Make this partly meditation for the purpose of receiving instructions, and then balance it with prayer (Love source) to create the needed energy. Do not waste time setting up institutions with structures, membership and business. Keep the organization to a minimum and stress the work! This is critical.

Teachers

Pay special attention to those coming into balance for the first time! There will be many, due to my work. Teach the new ones about who they are and how they can have peace of mind and how they can love themselves through the recognition of the entity they really are. Psychological balance will result with spiritual enlight-enment. Make a place in your teachings for simplicity. Remember that who you are now is a result of many years of gradual discernment, and that the new ones cannot absorb this all at once. They will come because of the love they feel... drawn to the new consciousness. Always remember that your primary efforts are to teach balance through love. It is not necessary to teach them the universal "workings of things" as you know them. Let them leave in peace without forcing anything on them. They will have enough balance to continue. Some will remain with you for further training so they can join the transmutation efforts.

For the enlightened give the message of the new alignment and what it means, including <u>all</u> the messages contained here.

Teach tolerance of the human process! This alone will create more transmutation of negative to positive than almost anything you can do. Tolerance is a result of love balance. Use the tolerance yourself to keep clear. Celebrate those other teachers who also are receiving information, and do not ever feel that you are less than any other. New information will occur simultaneous to many, and is never proprietary.

> **IMPORTANT:** Teachers – your tools will not be accurate for long! Those of you involved in using any predetermined systems of universal rules and laws must adjust your charts. I will give you more information on this in the next message. Also, you must realize that your new powers for these times will allow any balanced entity to leap beyond the karmic overlay and any other predetermined magnetic birth implant. This new power is significant, and you can use it to remove obstacles in your path and to live a much longer life.

Healing

Heal the sick. You are not to be denied this process, and it has been available to you for years. Many of you are doing this now, but none of you are claiming the love God-Source with the results that other religious leaders have. Show the power! It's for all. Heal the sick by balancing the organs. The love God-Source will respond if appropriate.

I have already given my partner more information on how this healing process works, but here are the basics: The best method is one-on-one. Your spiritual entity must communicate directly on a spiritual level with one other entity. There will be instant, logical communication from the clear, balanced one to the physically unbalanced one about the permission to move beyond karma and use the 'action window' available. If appropriate, the unbalanced one will receive physical balance, and will be healed. It's that simple! Remember that everything is in its place. Some will come to you for healing because it really is their moment for it. They are there by design to receive it. It is your responsibility to take your power to help fulfill their purpose. It is all interrelated. Others will come who are not ready yet. They have more work to do, and that might include remaining sick. It is not for you to know this. Take responsibility only for the healing process. Do not take responsibility for what appears to be a failed healing. This is up to God, not you. Be aware: Do not limit the healing you ask for. The love source has no limitation. It is possible to create matter where none was before... to reconnect biological pathways, or to simply balance the system for better health. Your "miracles" are logical applications of the love God-Source. They are appropriate and are scientific. When you learn about transmutation of matter, you will know what I mean. Your magic today will be the commonplace of tomorrow. Use the power!

Experience The Gift

On a personal level learn to "feel" or experience the Love source at any time you wish. <u>This is your new right</u>. It will create the peace you will need to walk through what is to come. From your awakening in the morning to your retirement at night you can have this with you at all times. Imagine what this can mean for you! The more time you spend experiencing this, the easier it will be for you to be a clear channel for our information, for your teaching and prayer and healing.

Your word love <u>is now</u> appropriate in the context of the "feeling." The Love of God is not a new feeling to humans. It is exemplified in the scriptures in the 13th chapter of the first book of the Corinthians. It is the feeling of a loving parent who takes care of all your needs. It is the feeling of a loving friend or mate who loves you unconditionally. It has substance and is thick. It is the loving arms of God. It can actually be seen by some. It is of singular source, and is unique in the universe. It belongs to us all, and is our personal source and our gift all at the same time.

When you experience it, you are feeling not only the comfort and warmness of peace from the universe, but the love and admiration of the collective entities of the universe, all who know who you are and congratulate you for your perseverance to have read this message and have taken its communication seriously.

I AM Kryon.

Chapter Two

The New Energy

Teachers...

How does it serve you to reject change?

Have you worked on the path for so many
years just to reject your gift?

You are needed now more than ever
to show the way to the new ones
who are infants in the work.

You won't be able to do it alone any more...
...so you'll have to have tolerance for the others.

We will support you....
and love you...

...and give you the peace that
you are missing.

From the writer... (again)

What you are reading now is being written starting on the fourth day of the beginning of 1992. What you just read was written in the beginning of December, 1991. This is significant, and will set a time frame for you when Kryon speaks of 'now."

From my standpoint, it is obvious that from now on Kryon wishes to speak in the "first person" state that you just experienced, and this is the way I shall continue to honor the request for communication. I will also occasionally place comments in *italics* in parentheses when I feel it is needed for clarity. This will differentiate Kryon's immediate thought group translation from my review translation.

This next section is a continuation of what you just read... Although Kryon spoke of 'more to come' during the last session, there seemed to be no more communication, and I felt that I was finished with the writing. Now I know better.

The book continues, but it had to wait to be channelled within a specific energy, that being 1992. This next part is more for teachers of all kinds within the Metaphysical belief system; but even if you are not a teacher, please continue. There will be information for you as well.

These writer remarks are obviously written prior to the channelling, and I have chosen to keep it this way, rather than editing it after the information is given. So you can share in the 'liveness' of this experience along with me.

You might wonder if the organizational headings are added later, after the channelling. The headings are supplied and organized at the time of writing, and very little is changed after the fact.

What follows from here will again be as fresh to your mind as it will be to mine.

Kryon Channellings
Chapter Two

The New Energy
Timing and Power

Greetings! I am Kryon, of magnetic service. Each one of you is loved dearly! Indeed this communication is special. Everyone receiving this now will be doing so in the new energy, and I have withheld communicating it before now so you would better understand. I was not even able to give this information to my partner until now, due to the timing involved.

As I previously communicated, I have been here since 1989. I have a support group of my own which is currently in the orbit of your planet Jupiter. Their main support for me is that of energy and resources for my work. Although I am the magnetic master, my work can hardly be done alone! Some of you may have already seen them as they occasionally come and go from the important areas where they are helping me set up. They have been here for 11 full years as of this date, and they will continue 11 more with me.

The time duration of my work is important for you, so you can realize exactly what is taking place, and also take advantage of your new action opportunities.

It has taken three years of preparation for the opening of your year 1992. January 1, 1992 marked the year of the change, continuing through the eleven year progress to its prospective completion on the date December 31, 2002. I will not be here past that time. Many have speculated and written about an 18 to 20 year cycle. This is misinformation. My task will take no more than a total of 14 years, three of which have already passed, bringing for you a very important and significant time on Earth.

Make no mistake; I am the one you expected. I am the one chosen with the responsibility to realign your grid system, allowing for remarkable changes in your power.

I communicate now directly to the teachers. Many of you are becoming uncomfortable now. Some of you who are understanding what is about to happen are finally <u>becoming</u> comfortable. What a dichotomy!

This section is specifically for <u>all</u> of you, so you can understand what you are feeling and what to do with it. Also I will try to impart the opportunities of a brand new power you have... how it works, how to use it, and the pitfalls of asking for it.

The Systems Workers

Are you a worker in systems? I have already spoken of some of your human implants at birth. The biggest set of implants are really '**imprints**' that come in with you from your last incarnation(s). These include karma, astrological presets, life lessons (related to karma), magnetic field patterns (*auric life colors*), star karma and many more (but I have itemized the strongest lot). Each human body also has polarity balances which are distinctive for the individual lessons yet to be learned.

Many of you work with these systems, and have become very proficient in their use. Information has been given to you through the years that could only have come from my side of the veil for use in these Metaphysical techniques. Astrology, for instance: This science is truly that! I have already given you a glimpse of what your magnetic field is doing for your life force and your spirituality, and I have also informed you that gravity is a portion of the equation (this is why the placement of your moon affects your emotions). Consider for a moment the effects on your Earth gravity from the other celestial bodies around you. Your solar system in particular (and your galaxy in general) actually 'couch' your Earth's magnetic system, and therefore your spirituality. It is all related, and that is the study of astrology... how these other celestial bodies work to affect you personally. This is just one example of an imprint. You are born into a specific spiritual energy, created by the alignment of the magnetics around you, and it has a predictable effect on you from then on. This would be very similar to a hardy tree or plant taking seed and growing up in a tropical area on Earth. If it travels, it will be happiest in the same kind of environment it grew in, although it could live almost anywhere. And you could predict that when the elements got hot or wet, the plant would be happier. In cold or drought it would be less productive. This is simple information, where you predict items about the behavior of a living thing by having knowledge of its seed conditions, but seldom is it applied in respect to the position of the planets in relation to humans, except by those who understand that it is so. This, then, would be a systems worker in astrology.

Some of you work with the body's magnetic field. This could either be in actual healing work, or in the study and teaching of auric colors and patterns and their meaning to the individual. You are also systems workers, since you depend on birth imprints, and work with predictable factors.

If you use charts of any kind, or refer to tables when you work, you are a systems worker. Even those of you who deal in karmic awareness use rules for those you are helping. If you deal with past life regression, birthing and re-birthing, or reading life lesson imprints, you are using the systems.

For all of you, there will be tremendous change in relation to your work. **Please do not fear it**. You are loved, and congratulated for your work! In general it may continue as before, but there are some items to take into consideration, and one item in particular to realize and look for (*to be explained shortly*). I can guarantee that <u>all of you</u> are uncomfortable right now! If you are a systems worker and you are not uncomfortable with today's energy, then you either know the information I am about to give you, or you have lost your balance and are just existing within the framework of the system without awareness or enlightenment.

Your uncomfortable feelings come from the fact that you are the spiritual leaders, and yet something has shifted that is telling you intuitively that your powers are different. Some of you have already noticed an alarming fact (but you are not sharing it yet): that suddenly your systems are not as accurate as they have been in the past. You may feel that you are losing your power (a very distressing feeling)! Even though this is a positive, powerful time for you, the uncertainty of what you are observing is affecting your personality through fear.

This is important for you: You have lost nothing but your system alignment. And (most important) you have an exceptional opportunity as you read and understand this to do something previously unavailable to you or any human since your Earth history began.

My grid change is skewing your charts. In the year 1992 those of you using any kind of planetary system references must consider realigning them 2 to 3 degrees to the right (as you view them) during the year. Since this is fairly vague, for verification and accuracy covertly do overlays that only you are aware of that reflect this, and compare them to the reality of the life process around you – and especially to the people that you are trying to help and heal. Anchor any geographical or Earth time references in the identical manner that you already have been doing. Change only the non-Earth aspects. I cannot at this time give you an actual time frame for the full three-degree shift, since you as humans now control my work. I respond to your transmutation work with appropriate shift, so I am unable to be specific since I do not have knowledge of how you will fare. The shift will not be any greater than three degrees in 1992, but it is greater than one degree at this time.

Changing the non-Earth aspects of your charts may seem backwards from what has actually happened, but to your systems it will appear correct. The difference is that <u>Earth</u> changed... and nothing else around it did. An analogy to this would be: If you are sitting very still on a rotating chair (*piano stool*) being fed by a giant mechanical robotic machine assembly, and suddenly something rotates the chair to the left, the big machine (*unaware that your stool moved*) will miss your mouth from then on and you will have to change something to correct it, or you won't be able to live. It is far easier to move your head and body slightly to the right to compensate for the chair rotation than to try to move the giant machine.

Non-Systems Workers

If you are a 'see-er,' that is, a person who works almost entirely with psychic abilities, you are a non-system worker. This applies to 'see-ers,' channellers and readers of all kinds (tarot & rune, etc.), where the information given is pertinent to the moment, and is not developed from past experience or patterned, universal information. The reason the tarot and runic readings are non-systems is because they do not relate to each other as an integrated, relational group until they come together <u>at the moment</u> to form a current spiritual picture. They are really signposts, with group interactions and interpretation.

You see-ers should be feeling good. In fact, you should be noticing a positive change for the better... when all around you things are in transition! My alignment will agree with you, since you are experiencing greater sight and accurate readings. My alignment is correct for this, and you will enjoy even greater success in your work from now on. You also have a great opportunity, however, to change your life in a spectacular way.

For Those Caught in the Middle...

My dear ones! Those who are both systems workers and see-ers, please take heart. The internal confusion you are experiencing is **false**. The fear you feel is unwarranted, and before you finish this communication you can arise with full power as never before. This is the singular love message I bring to all of you.

The Great New Power

For all of you (*all humans*) there is new, important information: With the beginning of this eleven year cycle, you have the power to transmute your imprints (*not implants*). Never before has this been available to any human unless they have arrived with no implants or imprints (such as Jesus). This has a tremendous impact on both your personal lives and your work. First you must understand what this actually means, and how you can have it, and keep it. Second, you must realize how it is going to impact your work.

Let me attempt to be clearer on this new revelation. Here is where I trust my partner to be very careful in his translation. You have earned a new powerful attribute that is directly related to your performance on the Earth plane. My arrival and subsequent grid re-alignment work is a "handshake" to your performance. It is not an event to be feared or distrusted. Those of you in tune with the cosmos in any way will know that this time has been foretold under many names and in many cultures... and it's here. My communications about the end times in the last section stopped short of the important good news for <u>those who are balanced</u>. How would you like to void all the karma that you have been working through all your life? Would you like to be another aura color, or be free of a fixed attribute? Are you tired of your astrological sign? Are you bored with working through a life lesson? These questions are tremendously significant!

With karma comes health problems, unexplained fears and troubles, monetary problems, human relationship workouts and career puzzles. Karma also brings prosperity, health, wisdom, manifestation and abundance (such is the duality). Life lessons (related to karma) are superimposed. They are overall imprints that set a covert (*commonly unrecognized*) goal for you to work toward. As described earlier, your astrological identity is a 'seed' imprint that is supposed to help you with timing along your way. Also important is that the place on Earth where you are, and the people you work with, are part of your karma group system. Also, something not well understood on Earth is your star karma. Not all of you have expressions on Earth each time. There are many of you that come and go from other areas of the universe, with different sets of learning parameters. This star karma is often heavy. Would you like to be free of the imprint? As mentioned, there is duality in all this, good and bad depending on your individual path. What will it mean to be free?

In the last section I spoke of the healing process. You will recall that it was related to karma and the overall imprint. All human diseases, dysfunctions and imbalances are directly related to karmic imprint. Without any karmic imprint you would have no health problems at all. One of the reasons that your great historic characters in ancient times seemed to live so long is that they carried no karmic imprint. Many were 'first timers' without any karma. There are very few of those now, since your lessons have been in progress for enough time for multiple expressions to have occurred, building up the 'textbook' of lessons to be experienced, and complex imprints.

Through the new love energy you now have the ability to claim this new power, and to actually leap over your karma and all your action windows directly to a place of neutrality. This neutrality voids the process of duality, erases the need for lessons, <u>assumes a graduation status</u> and provides for tremendous power. I will describe to you what this will mean for you directly; then I will admonish you to consider the potential challenging factors as well. Make no mistake: this new power will be necessary for you to do the transmutation work for the Earth. The Earth <u>will need</u> many of you to make this jump; otherwise there will not be enough power necessary to accomplish the task at hand for the next 11 years.

Many events will happen for you with this leap to a neutral imprint. I will list a few of the processes later, but first I must clarify what it will mean for you to be 'graduate status.' Graduate status normally means that you are ready to leave. Simply put, you have no more lessons and you are finished here. Now, however, this status is available to you early... you have earned it, and it is **no longer associated with leaving**. After you have made the change to this new status, you will be different. Your life will be changed, and you will feel different. All the changes will eventually be positive, but like any change there will be a period of adjustment. After the adjustment you will still be yourself, but with no past imprint, and with no goal imprint. This is going to take wisdom and understanding, tolerance and love.

Your personality can remain the same, as you choose. Whatever the best parts of life you perceive will remain yours. The parts you always wished could change, can now do so. This is where the power lies. You now have a <u>direct path</u> to the singular love power source that only is possible through graduation status. Jesus had this status (and more), and He spoke to you of this. He also told you that you had the power to obtain the status also, to be as He was (*John 1:11-12*). Here it is! ... and you need it to help change the Earth. You also will have a much longer life. Your aging will slow, and disease may not attach itself to you. In addition you will be able to 'pass' all items internally that might otherwise affect you. Up to this point the items that were taken into your body were examined by your karmic imprint through your basic genetic code (your biological imprint and your spiritual imprint are within the same structure). If your karmic imprint matched the overall result of the substance, then it was accepted or rejected. This 'pass or fail' routine was carried out for good and bad substances, thereby controlling if you got disease, good or bad nourishment, fast or slow metabolism (*thin or fat body*), acceptance or rejection to medicine, vitamins and health remedies. It also could protect you from, or allow for cancer, heart disease, high blood pressure, and so on. It controlled your life span (unless it was to terminate in other ways), and made an impact on how you looked. It also allowed you various talents. (All talents are possible with a neutral imprint.) As I previously mentioned, implants (not imprints) are most often given to restrict your understanding, or your abilities. Your implant structure will change (more on this later) to allow for expanded understanding and talent. You will be unaffected by energies around you. You will no longer absorb negativity, but will transmit positive energy wherever you go, an aggressive rather than protective posture. Foods that previously gave you rashes, allergies, or simply made you ill, will no longer affect you. You will still be challenged with common sense nutrition, but the items that affected you differently than most will no longer do so. Disease will ignore you unless you specify otherwise. Accidents will be reduced, and abundance will flow as needed.

Does this sound fantastic? Perhaps you do not believe it. Know this: the words on this page are for you. You are not reading this by accident. Only the correct situation allowed this writing to reach you, and now you have the responsibility of action or non-action.

Either way your life will be changed because you have seen the truth. If you love a certain kind of food, and 'by accident' you find out that the food is made from something unusual, it forever will change the way you think about the food. You may still eat and enjoy it, but your knowledge and wisdom about the truth of its origin will never go away.

Why Wouldn't You Want it?

Having a neutralized imprint will bring about changes that you have never experienced before. You will have temptations that you never had before, and things will change for you that may seem difficult. In addition the period of adjustment may not be pleasant.

(1) Since birth you have been accustomed to behaving a certain way. Your speech, desires, actions and defenses have all been shaped through karma. Someone speaking angrily to you evoked anger... being accused brought defense... your personality 'buttons' were regularly pushed, and an expected reaction resulted. These items are karmic, and are also tied to your imprint. Why are some people angry all the time? Why are some people peaceful? These are all controlled from your imprint. Quite often your karma is structured to help you get through some of these feelings, and learn wisdom and peace by voiding the fear. Fear therefore is <u>allowed</u> to be with you by way of your imprint; but peace is the natural state, and you possibly had to work for it.

Your personality therefore will change. Universally it will be for the better, but it will make you seem different from others. A person angry at you will evoke no angry reaction, but at the same time you will lose a part of you that has become very comfortable. Peace is natural; but it may seem boring if you have had a life of drama and intensity, or were used to creating it for yourself.

(2) The biggest temptation you will have is one you never even considered: you will be able to leave without pain. You will be able to simply disappear and leave. This will be intuitive to you, and the process will be clear. Why not? You will have the power and the permission to do so, and in the past when you reached this point... you did! Why stay and work when you are allowed not to? The answer is obvious. Suddenly you have new permission to stay and **use your power to change the planet**. Your permission to leave is absolute, and would result in no negative energy, but you will also have a feeling of renewed responsibility to stay and help the Earth in a way that is grand. Remember in my last communication I told you that you are the ones most respected among entities. Those of us in service honor and love you dearly for your work! Someday when you reach my side, your graduation will be most glorious. When you finally arrive, you will again have a complete grasp on what you really have been doing for the universe, and how your actions have helped us all. With all this, can you really stay and do the work? Yes! But consider your determination before you ask for this status. You will receive help (*more on this to come*), but the temptation could be strong.

(3) The karmic group you are with will no longer be linked to you. This might be the most painful of all for you. Many of your friends, or even your mate, could forsake you. To them you will have changed and become someone else, even if that someone is more understanding and tolerant. Love (*The singular source*) is perfect, and in that realm it sees these things as perfect, just as it sees appropriate death as perfect. For you, however, the human bond will be missed. This is part of the adjustment period. Are you capable of being alone if necessary? You might not find a partner quickly who has made the same commitment. Please consider this. It would be far better for you to continue as you are, in love and understanding, doing your best with the amount of enlightenment you now enjoy, than to make the status change and become lonely. Even other humans with enlightenment may forsake you due to ego karma.

(4) EGO will be your worst enemy. To some degree your ego was contained or unleashed by your imprint. Even Jesus had some problems with ego when He realized His power at certain times in His life, and grew impatient with those who were unenlightened. EGO is intrinsically human. It is not a consideration on this side of the veil. I speak of the self-importance that a biological mind conceives by itself. Ego is what happens when the greater is around the lesser. This is never the case with my side of the veil. There is no 'lesser' here. Human ego is an unwarranted feeling of power, and it is as a drug to the human mind. In fact you will have to have an additional implant (*more on this*) to block it from affecting you past the point where you can maintain control. Although imprints affect a great deal, there are common biological systems in every human that must be considered in all of this, such as ego, sexual lust or hunger ... constant irritations to the higher self, but things that are biological, and therefore items that must be balanced. Being human requires some ego just to deal with other humans; but in your case you actually will be more powerful than most, and the ego reaction will be very strong.

Ego displaces love, and if you become egocentric, then the balance necessary to maintain your status will be lost. I have yet to describe to you the consequences of this. You must remain balanced.

(5) At the same time, you must assume an aggressive spiritual nature. Let me explain. Especially for those of you who are enlightened, I guarantee you will relate to this. Have you been protective in any way of your psyche in social situations where you have to interact with other humans? Have you taken precautions to protect your energy from being diluted? Have you ever felt as though your energy was violated, and therefore you had to bring yourself 'up' again to the higher vibration that you were before the violation? Do you use amplifiers where you live to help the vibration stay high? When you touch strangers, do you consciously

think of how their energy is going to affect you? Are you concerned about these things?

This nature is a <u>defensive</u> one, and is no longer appropriate! Until now it may have been necessary for you to do this to remain at the vibration you desired, but now you must abandon this stance! You no longer have to worry about any other lower vibration affecting you. Can you do this? This is a mental change that may be very difficult indeed. Think of Jesus as He walked among the people, touching them, healing them and speaking to them. Think of the way He sought out the unenlightened and gave them power. He was always on the aggressive, that is, He gave power instead of losing it, and this is how you must be. This is not to be confused with being evangelistic. This is only in reference to your own power and its balance with those around you.

When you touch someone, they will receive <u>from you</u>... period. There will no longer be any flow of negative to positive regarding your power. Your balance will void that condition. You will never have to fear a lower vibration interfering with your own. Those with lower vibrations will be changed simply by being around you, even without your thinking about it. Your amplifiers will no longer be necessary for you (but still might be appropriate for those living or visiting with you). In a teaching capacity you will have many coming and going who will still benefit by your former energy-changing devices; but <u>you</u> simply will not need them. In addition you will be able to charge those devices yourself! You will become as a generator of power and positive influence. Nothing will be able to penetrate your power. It is the singular love source that I have been speaking about, and it is absolute. Even those of you who do not change your imprint can now take advantage of this new condition. I will speak of this later.

(6) Another of the most difficult new adjustments will be in regard to your psychological attachment to the past. Please believe me when I tell you that this is not an enlightened characteristic, but a very human one. All of you up to now, as part of your imprint, view the past as somehow sacred. You revere family members who have passed on. You fantasize about events gone by; some of you actually save objects so that you can easily review past memories. These attitudes are negative and not enlightened, and are given to you so you can lift yourselves (*learn*) above them in your process of becoming balanced. When you are balanced, you become aware of the 'now' time frame more than ever. Events of your human past will become appropriately neutral to you. Family members that are no longer here will either be with you in spirit, or have long since returned within another incarnation. They are in the 'now' with you in your karma group in some fashion. This realization alone should give you a much better perspective of the present moment. Humans spend lifetimes learning to release memories and events; you will have it for the asking.

Preoccupation with trips into the past are an addiction with negative energies. These memories are used to bring you to a place of sadness, sorrow, longing and self-indulgence with pity. They are also used to create feelings of anger and unfulfilled retribution; all negative! Examine why you keep feelings from your past, and determine if any of this fits you.

Note: It is highly proper to honor and celebrate the past expression of a karmic group member. Is that the reason you have the past items? Or does it create a feeling of wishing for something else – whatever it is. Preoccupations with human heritage is almost meaningless, given the truth of the many expressions that each entity has. It is only a karmic tool for your growth. Keeping items for the purpose of honoring the entity's past expression is honorable. The difference between an enlightened past honoring and a human negative past retrospective is simple. Do you feel joy or sadness around the item? Joy is the only appropriate feeling.

You will be without past reflection. That is to say that your memory will be intact, but the feelings you expect to have as a human will not be there. This is going to seem strange to you. Did you really love your lost loved ones? If so, shouldn't you feel sorry they are gone? When you feel very little human sadness about them, you will have a tendency to question yourself. Are your feelings gone? No; only your imprint.

(7) Finally, the new overwhelming emotion that will be yours will be the new love vibration. This will seem 'heavy' to you, heavy in the terms of responsibility. You will indeed perceive the 'now' almost as I do, and with it will come an intense sense of responsible action. It isn't the 'free and easy' kind of emotion that you might have associated with love up to now. It is the kind of love you saw reflected in the face of Jesus. It is wise love, coming from a place that recognizes the soul of a person when you look at him. It is the beauty of a dream only imagined, wrapped in the gauze of honor and tied with the joy of new birth. There is no frivolity in these new feelings. These represent the wise feelings that truly understand and celebrate appropriate death, as well as appropriate life. You will find yourself grown up. Is this really for you?

The Adjustment & Help

When you make this shift, you are going to need help. This is where those of us in service come in. We will recognize when you are ready (*more on this later*). It is going to be necessary for you to receive at least one new implant (not to be confused with imprint), and a change of guides. Let me be clear on each.

I spoke earlier regarding the implants to your human mind. These spiritual implants basically are designed for human restriction. They restrict the true realization of your soul, as well as your understanding of how the spiritual balances with the physical to create full science (*miracles*). Without these implants, there would be no tests and no learning. When Jesus walked the Earth, he was sent without an imprint and without human implants. This made Him much different than any other human. He was here as a master to teach. He knew it, and the only difficult items He really had to deal with were biological, and common to all. He felt emotions, drives, pain, ego and fatigue, just like everyone, but He did not have a set of implants, restricting the veil.

Implants are spiritual restricters that keep your soul entity from playing an active part. They are given at birth and they never change unless those in service change them. Many times new restrictors are given when a person has reached a certain point in his growth to warrant it. You do not have the power to change an implant/restrictor, and it is appropriate that this is so. An example of when an implant is changed by itself is when a person moves through an action door and successfully moves past a karmic attribute. When this happens you actually change your vibration, and also your imprint. If this were not so, you would have retained the karmic characteristic even though you had worked through it. (Not quite fair, wouldn't you say?) This actually changes your genetic code magnetic balance (DNA).

When you shift to graduate status <u>you must have a major new implant, or release of the old</u>. It is offered to void your old karma (all of it). This is the mechanics of the transformation, and it involves those in service who do these tasks. You probably are aware already of those in service around you who are your 'guides'. Some call them angels, and this is also appropriate.

To us their energy packages are instantly recognizable as those in service for the individual entity path in lesson.

You are much like an Earth athlete in training. There is a support group around you, in various hierarchies of service. The ones that are closest to you are your guides. The farthest from you are those like my entity, who deal with the mechanics and maintenance of the school. Each of you currently has <u>two guides</u> with you. These belong to <u>no one</u> else. These are not entities that sit in judgment of you, or watch you for evaluation. They are spiritual servants and helpers. Some of them are between incarnations, and therefore they are not always in service (*guide service*). Some are masters of this service and will always be guides. This is the way of it, and its explanation as to why must wait for your passing, for it is not pertinent in any way to your path at this time.

Perhaps many of you have been aware of the guides, but you perceive more than two? Only a very few of you are given an adjustment to be able to discern the difference between the characteristics of veiled entities. Most of the time you are only aware of figures or shapes. You only have two personal guides, and the rest are usually peripheral entities that are there for numbers of reasons... none of which are wrong. Remember that I spoke of many other entities being on Earth in other expressions of learning? There is much coming and going that you are not necessarily aware of, but that occasionally becomes visible to you. It is simpler to identify what is yours rather than to explain what isn't. You have two guides who love you and are always there for you.

With your shift, you will have a major adjustment: you will lose one or both guides (depending on your path at that time), and <u>gain another</u>. You will be the only entities on Earth with three master guides (*there's that 3 again*). These are master guides, who will assist you in your task of teaching and transmutation of energy for the Earth. (A master guide is a guide that is always in service and never in lesson.) Even as I transmit this communication through thought groups to my partner, the master guides are assembling and are on the way to service for the Earth. There is great activity around your solar system. (Kryon Book Two - *Don't Think Like a Human*, offers proof of this! - page 228).

The guide change will accompany the implant adjustment all at the same time. If you thought you were sensitive, just wait! This has been described on other planets as the 'blackness.' There will be a period of time of about ninety days where you will be without the guides. You will have the feeling of having lost your best friend and your only child in the same moment! The departure of 'guides from birth' are deeply felt by the soul entity within you. I spoke of your soul entity earlier. Your soul entity is that part of you that is totally aware of both sides of the veil, but is kept from participating directly on Earth through your implants. It is always there, and is the part of you that is absolutely eternal. It knows me and I know it. It is very familiar with all your expressions, and it is that part of you which is human spirituality. It is also the part that is constantly prodding you to search for God. It has no gender. Since you have no direct communication with your own soul entity, you will not understand these feelings. They will not be explainable.

When the guides leave, the soul entity is alone. It has never been without the guides, and they have been in constant contact with it. These things may sound unbelievable to you (your implants are supposed to make it seem so), but they are the simple mechanics of your soul. The Master Jesus also had guides, and their removal before his vibrational shift on the cross caused him to cry out in confusion. Do you remember those words? They are recorded for you to examine. He experienced the withdrawal right before his change... just as you will.

There isn't a more empty feeling than when the guides leave. Even if one is going to remain, there is a period of time when there are none. The remaining one must move off for a time of adjustment. These guides represent the only contact with the pure love energy that exists for your soul. When they leave, you will absolutely feel it. Meditation will bring no solace. Centering will not work, and prayer will seem to bounce back from the sky. Again, when Jesus was suffering on the cross, He was temporarily removed from his guides. This is a common spiritual attribute - the dark before the light. It is in almost every spiritual writing on the planet, not just in your culture. It corresponds to a purification before the new energy arrives... and erasing of the old. It has to be this way, and you will find it throughout spiritual history. It might be very disconcerting and uncomfortable for you also. You will almost experience the sorrow of your own death, passing into blackness without a sense of hope. Be assured that this is in perfect order. Those who would tell you that this is not an attribute of God are misinformed about the way of love. Look for it!

I told you there would be pitfalls to your new power, and this is one of them. This is the fire before the peace. It is temporary, and you <u>will</u> be able to get through it. You **will not** be allowed to leave during this time; and although your guides are gone, some of the other entities less close to you are in the 'neighborhood' to watch out for you. They are not communicators, however, and you will have no awareness of them. Each of you will perceive this differently. If you are really prepared, then it will be expected, and therefore will seem more gentle. If you want advice to help you through this, then when you know it is beginning (and you will), preoccupy yourself with earthly tasks, concentrating on goal oriented work and the completion of something you enjoy. This is a diversion tactic for your soul, and will often work well for the adjustment period.

More help... I cannot stress enough how important faith will be at this time. If you make the shift, then find yourself changed... without your friends, with a mate who is confused, perhaps with no more vocation... what's left? The answer to this is simple: Everything you **never had** is left! You <u>will</u> <u>be</u> <u>cared</u> <u>for</u>! Your position will be honored. The three master guides, in combination with all the unseen entities around you that also are here to support you, will be in high gear to make certain that you will be served. Timing will still be very important, and so patience will be necessary. But your new status will allow for this, and you won't have trouble with the waiting. Fear won't play the part it used to, since you have the power to leave at any time you wish (hence the temptation to do so). You will carry with you your own temple. What this means is that you will be totally self-sufficient, spiritually, physically and mentally. Sustenance will be no problem, health will be no problem, and you <u>will</u> <u>not</u> be lonely. You will have too much joy to feel alone. Your new guides will often be visible to you with enough clarity for verification of their presence, but not much more. If you remain balanced, you will be happy and prosperous... believe it!

What if you fail?

It is felt by those in the universe that plan such things that many of you will fail, even after receiving the power of graduation status. This is not the first time a planet has come into this kind of vibration, or enlightenment, so there is precedent in the projection. This would mean that many will actually disappear and leave the planet after they receive the power. This would be for two reasons: (1) They desire it; that is, they wish to leave instead of staying to help. (2) They cannot remain balanced due to ego problems, or other human biological tendencies. The latter of these would be involuntary; that is, the entity would simply vanish if they became unbalanced enough.

There is no negative attribute to leaving the planet while in graduate status for whatever reason. Even if you fail to remain and help, and leave in an involuntary manner, you will generate no negative attributes in your passing. Your status is absolute, and will be celebrated as highly as one who stayed. This may not seem totally fair to you, but like the story that Jesus told of the prodigal child, who left and was extravagant – then came back and was honored by his father to the same degree of the son who did not leave – this is the way with the singular love source. Jesus taught much about this kind of love; perhaps with your new power in these new times a fresh look would be in order of the things Jesus spoke of, and the examples he gave. New knowledge and understanding may result from the reexamination of words from this teacher that we sent for your enlightenment.

What is Your Path Now?

Many of you reading this will not desire to follow this new power path, realizing that it is not yet your time to do so. Please do not feel 'wrong' if this is your realization. It is appropriate that you feel this way, and it is in deep wisdom that you should continue without this new status... knowing that you will be far better off, but can still do a great deal to support the ones who are going to need you during this time, while all of you are helping the planet. Individual discernment is very important in this self evaluation decision. You will impress no one if you decide to take this path, and you will disappoint no one if you do not. This is a decision based in the spiritual discernment of knowing where you are in your own path at this time.

Those of you who feel you are ready can proceed to the next step. You must prepare yourself mentally to be moved out of your existing situation, whatever it is. Things will change for you, and you must be accepting of this. Your earthly career or vocation that has allowed you to earn the monetary exchange necessary for you to have food and shelter may be terminated or changed. Your decision will be irreversible, and you cannot change your mind.

If you are prepared and wish to make the shift, then you must openly petition for it by verbalizing it to the universe. Many of you are so in touch with this side of the veil that this communication will be clear and immediate. For some, however, it will require a verbalization so all can hear you (*all spiritual entities*). Your intent is extremely powerful, and Spirit will know if it is pure. Don't ask casually, with an idea that if you don't feel something then you will try something else! With this process you will be asking for the shift, and will also be expected to do some work to move into a new vibratory rate. (Kryon Books two, three and six tell of the new gifts and tools that will be yours to work with... but work is required!)

The next event that will happen will be an instant evaluation of the appropriateness of the request. Please understand that all of you have the power to make this shift because of the new energy now. As I mentioned, you have earned the right. The evaluation from this side of the veil is not a judgment, but an assessment of what will be required in the way of karmic adjustment. If an entity of little expressive experience (*few past expressions, and a great deal of karma left*) is asking for the new power, then there will be a different kind of service necessary to accomplish the change.)

No one will be turned down, but the timing of the shift and the difficulty of the passage will be very different for each person. A teacher asking for the shift may receive it immediately, and with very little discomfort. An entity of little expressive experience might have to wait longer for the process to begin, and then may have difficulty getting through it. As mentioned before, **all will get through it**. This is a spiritual gift! Spirit is not going to abandon you during this time! We love you.

My shift of the Earth's magnetic alignment is ongoing for some year. It may be that 1992 is not correct for your request, but that 2000 is. Use your power of intuition and meditation to ask if this is appropriate or not. Spiritual questions of this sort are very important to Spirit. We will absolutely answer you!

How will you know if you are beginning to receive it? First expect very vivid dreams, sometimes with some sorrow feelings. Next will begin the start of what you may feel is a deep depression. As stated earlier, this is the unceremonious departure of your guides. The rest is as I have described, and should last about ninety days. After that expect your life to change. Those intertwined in your former karmic path will continue on their learning path without you. You will be finished with interacting with them. The universe may remove them from you accordingly, so that their lessons will not be disturbed and so you can go about what you contracted for. Others still in your contract of love will remain.

How to Use the Power...

In future communication I will be describing in detail the methods you can use to transmute the negative to positive for the benefit of the planet during these times. When you receive this new status however, you will have no problem knowing how to go about it. For now, however, I will give you a few admonitions.

Be aware of attracting followers! Jesus came to Earth to impart a powerful message about a new age of spiritual consciousness, where humans could at last carry around the entire enlightened power of their soul entity with them, and could finally contain the power of the love therein. What a powerful message this is! He did not want to be worshiped, and look what happened. His entire purpose of existence was to impart the new knowledge and wisdom about the way universal love really works. In the process, however, many fell at His feet and worshiped Him instead of taking what He said and applying it for themselves. As described in detail during earlier communications with my partner, much of Jesus' teaching was interpreted, re-interpreted, translated and re-worked to be slanted into making Jesus into a Deity. When He was with you, He made it clear that no individual could receive the new love source unless they went by His new knowledge. Instead, this information passed to you today as a message where you are instructed to worship Jesus in order to get to 'God.' This was not the intent, and clearly shows how the minds of humans have worked to forge truth into a mold that better fits what they expect, or want to hear (or what they wish to teach others for the purpose of manipulation). (*If you want to know more about what Kryon has to say about Jesus, please read Chapter 6 'The Metaphysical Christ.'*)

Dismiss your followers! Do not allow anyone to take your place. That is, no one can teach in your place or do your work for you. It requires your new power to do the work. Do not allow anyone to write your words, and then assign altered meanings to them. Stay clear of mass media. Remember that in mass media your messages are being sent one way. This isn't communication, and you are challenged in your new work to actual communication (*two-way*). Your work is much more one-on-one. There is no evangelistic message to be pushed to the masses in your work. Heal the planet and heal your fellow humans in relatively small groups. Be aware that in both cases there is a return communication in this process. The mechanics of healing and transmutation require a spiritual interchange. (This is the great new secret revealed!) Do not depend on transparent viewing. (*I think Kryon means that video and film is far more transparent, and isn't as able to contain the covert viewing of spiritual energy nearly as well as a meeting in person.*) Very few humans are given the gift of discerning spiritual emanations by long distance viewing. (*Again, in person is required.*) Also, do not concentrate on the numbers of those who are with you. Work simply, methodically, for the few or the many, with diligence.

The New Vibrations

For the teachers: You must now realize that you might be seeing those of graduate status, or partial status (going through the transition) from now on. How will you 'see' them? What will be their expression color, or their auric pattern? You are used to patterns that have been pre-set and consistent. Even the mixtures and anomalies have been fairly consistent.; and now there is a brand new set to contend with.

Here are some words of advice for you: for the systems workers, don't even try to do the work once you perceive the individual is what he is. You will know, because no reading will even come close to being accurate. In actuality there should be no reason whatsoever for you ever to be reading one of graduate status. Once into this status, the individual will not be foolish enough to request a systems reading, for the imprint is meaningless, and they understand this. Birth dates and former life colors are now neutral, and cyclical biological forces no longer apply. Your systems read imprint information, and there will be none to read.

For those of you who are not systems workers, you will perceive the new graduate status as glowing white. Both the auric color and the expression color will be either white transparent (no color) or neutral (blending with the cosmos). Those of you with great perception will certainly notice the energy of the three master guides! The power of the 'three' will be felt as 'action' within the subdued confines of wisdom within the individual humans. There will be a feeling of peace about them, and universal understanding. And as mentioned, the unusual love vibration they will bring with them (through their new guides) will also attract followers like a magnet.

Another situation to watch for will be that of those <u>born into this new age</u> (*anyone born after 1/1/92*). These individuals will have a new imprint pattern to allow them to be comfortable with my new alignment. This pattern is different than any you have seen before, and will be quite distinctive. Look for new patterns of red and red-brown in the auric, and a new dark, dark blue in the life emanation. There will be certain negative aspects of the charts that will no longer apply to these new ones, especially in regards to certain <u>smaller planet</u> retrograde mechanics that have commonly required watching in the past.

It's For Everyone

This new time is powerful for <u>everyone of enlightenment</u>. These messages have concentrated on those wishing to take all the honors offered, and so you may feel that you must remain the same, or were not included here. This is not so! Although you may not be asking graduate status, some of the same new powers are yours for the asking as well.

Be aware that the process of aggressive rather than defensive power <u>is yours immediately</u>. Claim it and use it now! (*See item 5 under 'Why wouldn't you want it' earlier.*) Project your bubble of power wherever you go, and watch the people change around you. Former negative energies will seem to bounce off your new bubble instead of penetrating as they did before. You will receive what you project, however; and if you choose not to believe this message, then your bubble will be non existent, and you will have learned nothing by reading this. You also have far greater healing power than you did before the 1992 energy, both for yourself and others.

It is now appropriate that I explain why it is that you are able to be aggressive rather than defensive. Up to now the positive and negative energies were neutral when combined. That is, there was no bias toward either. In your expression so far in this time, you undoubtedly were very aware of the negative, and intuitively became aware that you had to flush the negative energies in order to maintain balance... since every negative energy voided a positive one, and could upset you if you were sensitive. The balance between positive and negative is <u>no</u> <u>longer</u> <u>neutral</u>. The new power of the singular love source available to you has changed this, and you have earned a situation where the positive will win every time. Negative will no longer supplant or void the positive. Instead the positive will ignore it, for it now has power it did not have before. As mentioned, you earned this power through your work so far on this planet by raising the vibration to its current elevated level. With this new power comes change. And again, that is why I am here.

Some of you will also receive new guides and some new attributes of higher vibration, even though you did not volunteer for the shift. This is normal for your growth during this time. If you have a depression that is especially deep for a brief time, then consider that you have had a guide change. Although you were not left alone (as in the case of those asking for graduate status), the departure of a guide is significant to your soul <u>at</u> <u>any</u> <u>time</u>. Since you are not in touch with your soul entity, it cannot tell you why it is unhappy; but you feel the results of it just the same. You can't speak for your digestive organ either, but you know when it wants to be fed. It is a similar situation, only spiritual instead of physical.

The New Attitude

My final words to you are again about your response to the new energy, and more about what it means to all of you. Throughout my time here I will have a common message, and you will read it often if you follow these writings. The message isn't necessarily about my service, for thankfully I don't have to try to explain the mechanics of my work. My entire purpose for interrupting my partner's life at this time is to give you information about **yourself**.

Many of you are feeling anxious now. Some of you are reacting to the change simply because it is change. Part of your being a human is to fear change and desire stability. As you look out from your Earth, you see sameness and consistency. You apparently see an unchanging and dependable state within the items that you can look at and measure over time. This is really not the case at all, for the universe is constantly in transition, and you would be able to see this if you could see the whole picture. Change is actually the desired state, but it is difficult for you to go against the feeling of your human attributes.

Please have faith that the <u>changes</u> <u>are</u> <u>good</u> <u>ones</u>. Again, not all is what it seems. Trust the fact that my adjustments are appropriate for you and the planet, and relax and have peace with the Earth during this time.

With the new energy comes a much brighter picture of how things work. This can be equated to the veil lifting slightly so that you can now see clearer than before. Whereas the communications of the past were often cryptic, or in story form for your re-interpretation, they are now far more basic. Whereas before messages might have been incorrectly interpreted due to a thick veil, now they will be clear. Hopefully you can see this happening as you read these messages. I am the first of many who will be speaking to you in a much plainer and simpler fashion than before.

Some of you may have noticed that for the first time you can perceive or be 'in touch' with an emotional feeling from my side to your side. My communications should already be stirring feelings within you that perhaps you have not felt before in regard to those of us on my side. This is new. In the past the universe would speak of love, but might seem to be indifferent and literal. Now is the time for you to be able to reach through the veil and feel some of what I am speaking about. This is new, and should give you excellent insight as to the fact of how much you are loved.

Without exception everyone was aware of the love of Jesus the messenger. This is what separated Him in history from other masters. This love has always been, but is now ready to show itself as power for you in your time. Imagine the immenseness of space to be pure unconditional love, the love of a watchful and doting parent or partner. When Jesus entered your side, He came dripping with this power, and you were aware of it. This is the very same divine and power-filled love that now more freely flows between you and me, and between all entities of my side to your side. This is the very special new arrangement you have earned. This alone should give you peace and solace, even within the anxiety over the changes you feel.

When you are finished with this reading and you retire tonight, I challenge you with this exercise. I guarantee you will have results if you are sincere, for this is truth; and it will manifest itself as reality because of that. You will feel some of this new love energy that I so often speak about. Please do the following.

The exercise: With your eyes closed, imagine yourself standing on a hill overlooking water. There is no noise except that of waves or wind. Stay there until you void your mind of everything earthly. If sounds or music will help, then sing to yourself in your thoughts to allow for peaceful thoughts. Slowly imagine the veil of duality approaching you, and stopping just a meter or so before you. If you cannot imagine this, then call for it and it will come. It has to come when called. Now stretch out both hands as in a welcoming fashion to your guides on the other side of the veil. You can do this actually, or just in your imagination, but keep your hands outstretched and wait. In a few moments you will feel your hands become warm, or tingle slightly. This is the truth of your hands being held! In addition, you will be aware of an overwhelming sensation that will make you weep. This sensation is one of joy and peace. The universe is really there, and it cares about you. You will be actually reaching through the veil, and can touch your guides. Your guides are your closest entities in service, and they love you dearly. They are there in <u>love service</u> and will be very receptive and excited to communicate with the 'rest of you' for the first time. Imagine their feelings, that you would respect them enough to reach out to them, for to them <u>you are the exalted one</u>, and they are serving you.

Pause and revel in this feeling as your hands are being held, for through your imagination you are actually creating <u>thought energy</u> which allows for this new communication. Thoughts are real energy, and what you will experience is very real and not just in your own mind. While you are in this state of joy, all fear will vanish about anything earthly, and a 'love wash' will take place that will provide you with peace and wisdom about the events you must face during your expression. You may even feel that you are beginning to rise above the land. Do not allow for this contact more than about <u>three minutes</u>, for to do more will fatigue your soul and translate to you as mental strain the next day. Believe me, you will be aware of the contact for hours. The after-glow will stay with you. Do not do this more than <u>one time a day</u>. This is not a mental exercise for the purpose of a positive feeling. What you are doing will be as real to you as anything you do during the day.

If I could leap off this page and appear to you at this moment, the first thing I would wish to do would be to honor you in some way, and to a biological human, this would be to hug you. If I do appear to some, I will restrain myself out of wisdom, lest I cause harm (which would be the case). You are all dearly loved without measure. My service to you as Kryon is first to love you, then to serve you through my magnetic knowledge. The priority of every entity of the universe revolves around the singular love energy source. The messages contained here are not simply empty, bare rules set out by the universe for you to follow to save the Earth. These messages are given by your spiritual family to improve your expression while on Earth, and to help you celebrate your newly gained power. The phrase 'heavenly father' was hardly accidental, for this is the very feeling of family you should have for those of us on this side of the veil. We are not indifferent to your work, and up to now it was very difficult, if not impossible, to impart that.

I am Kryon of magnetic service. Think of me when you are in doubt or in fear. Your thoughts can be transmuted into peace, and by your thinking of me, you can actually activate your guides into service. This is the way it works with thoughts. Prayer is much the same kind of thing. The actual mechanics of this is very complex, and it contains processes that are not within your ability at this time to absorb, due to the appropriate design of your implants. Trust me and accept the knowledge that your thoughts are active and can change things. You might wonder how one entity could 'hear' the thoughts of a multitude of humans simultaneously. Can you hear more than one sound at once, or do you have to ask them to wait in line? Is there a limit to the number of instruments that you can hear at once? It is much like this. Also remember that for each human, there are at least two more entities that do nothing more than wait for your thoughts and verbalizations!

The new love source is the great 'I AM,' the sun within the sun, and the center of all power. It is singular, and it belongs to all of us. I honor my partner for the clarity of this translation, and for not hesitating to write the thought images as they landed... for some are difficult, in that they might eventually bring ridicule from teachers and non-teachers alike.

> You have read the truth today. Some day it will shine so bright that you will wonder how you ever doubted any of it. I am Kryon of magnetic service. You all are dear!

Kryon

January 1992

There is joy and peace in your future when you
learn to harness the new power that is personally yours.

You have no idea what you can have until
you truly experience it.

...then you will wonder why you spent
so much time and energy
in the dark...

We love you.

Chapter Three

The First Live Channel

Kryon Channellings
Chapter Three

The First Live Channel

A personal message from the writer...

The time is March 3, 1992, 7 P.M., in Southern California. Seated before me are fourteen disciples of the new age. These people were invited by Kryon to witness the first attempt at a directly *live* channel. The following is the story of how this came to be, and the actual transcription of the message.

It is important, before I continue, to be certain that you have read the other chapters before this one. The chronology of the Kryon papers is becoming significant, and Kryon depends upon our earthly linear time frame for the logic of learning. That is, Kryon knows how we think, and has structured the information and teachings in a linear fashion, one foot before the other. So you need to be aware of the value of reading the information in the order in which it was given. I continue with my story.

Christmas 1991 was on the very edge of bringing in the new energy for the Earth. During that time I finished what I thought to be the Kryon writing. As you now know (if you have been following the readings), it turned out to be only the beginning. During this time (while in the shower) I had a clear message that I was to attempt a live channel event. I was mortified. Those who know me know that I depend on being totally prepared for everything. I get up early just to be certain that my alarm is set to wake me up. I prepare notes for everything, and then duplicate them in triplicate and place them in various pockets so that they can't be misplaced.

To put myself into a place where I have no notes and no agenda is to place myself into a bad dream, one where I speak slowly, don't say anything, and my feet go a mile-a-minute while traveling nowhere... in a stadium filled with people staring at me in my underwear while I try to get away.

The Kryon information is far more important than my ego. In fact, my life itself pales in contrast to the emmenseness of the message before me. I know that many are receiving this information now, so I'm hardly the lone messenger; but I'm here doing this because Kryon has made it clear that it is appropriate that it be so. This understatement is the Kryon way of saying that it is correct, proper, timely... , and anyway, I agreed to do it , remember? Kryon always wants me to *remember.* (as though I had all those billion-year-old communications with the master on the tip of my brain. Frankly I have a hard time remembering what I had for lunch last Thursday).

All right... I'll do it (I tell Kryon in my shower). I'll schedule a live channelling. I'll show up for several people and see what happens. If it has merit, I might even write it down. How about we start with my wife and two of my close friends, my cats and my bird? Perhaps we can serve several glasses of wine beforehand (not to the pets), and have a great time. (Can you tell the extent of my fear?)

Well, no such luck. Kryon wanted me to go to right to the Metaphysical Olympics! I'm supposed to go find the highest Meta-physical professionals and workers in the city, numbers of people I don't know, and channel for them! (Kryon told me in the shower.) I can't believe it. I have visions of them holding up cards with my score on it... and I end up with a collective 1.3 on a scale of

9. I even see some minus numbers on the cards. Kryon might as well have asked me to build an ark... or go see Pharaoh to "let my people go." I could tell that this was not going to sit well with my life lesson (*don't let anything define me*).

So I got to thinking: what's the worst that could happen? Grown-ups snickering while I grope and stammer for words given by a magnetic master from the spirit world that speaks to me almost every waking hour... except right at that moment? What if I'm too nervous to translate properly, and I tell them that meteors will fall in April unless they smoke clothespins? That's it... I can't do it... and no more showers either.

So... Kryon says to me (while in my car), "I'll do it for you; just give them the papers and wait." So in the latter part of February I sought out my trusted friend Barbra (who also happens to be a Metaphysical teacher of the highest order). In between appoint- ments she saw me, and I sheepishly told her my story. She accepted the challenge – no questions asked. I gathered copies of the Kryon communications, duplicated 14 sets, took them to Barbra, and waited to be called if the group wanted to hear more. Needless to say, the papers were well received. The group wanted to see me March 3 at 7 P.M..

I grew up a lot in the two weeks before the channel. I realized that I had to call for an implant to help balance me, and I did. I also felt a responsibility to be peaceful and joyful about the experience, and just let it happen. I realized that if I could release all the fear and anxiety over something like this, I could do it with anything in my life, no matter how severe. Then I realized what was really happening: Kryon had created a custom "fire walk" for me, and when it was done, everyone would win. If the group was really who they were supposed to be, then they would recognize the entity for what it was. They would enjoy the moment with me, celebrate the information (if any), and they would not judge me at all, but using their experience, assist me for the future. How obvious this is now!

I am seated in front of fourteen Metaphysicians, including the teacher Barbra and her husband, the teacher Michael. Among the twelve others are several full time Metaphysicians (earning their living doing the work), including numerologists, and psychics. Some are professional people who also work in Metaphysics, and there is at least one or two trained trancemediums. To my right sits my wife Jan, who is absolutely necessary as my anchor. I am oddly peaceful. The moment has arrived. My nervousness shows briefly in the flutter of my voice, and then Kryon takes over. I find myself doing something familiar: just translating the thoughts as they come flying in, trying to keep up with the flow, but at the same time being very aware of the extra energies before me.

What follows is the transcription of those thoughts and words as they happened. In addition, I have asked Kryon to add to the thoughts in a postscript manner, almost like a channel on top of a channel. This will be helpful, since (1) I discovered that during a live channel some explanation is left out. I believe this is due to the fact that some information is absorbed by those in attendance through communications with the higher self. When transcribed literally to paper, it seems to lack clear understanding... and (2) This was my first attempt at channelling the Kryon energy. And regardless of what anyone might tell you, I was nervous, and this had an effect on what may have been left out. To really clarify what happened, I have asked Kryon to "fill in the blanks" where appropriate. Those areas will be interspersed throughout the transcription in *italics*. Nothing has been left out, but thankfully Kryon has enhanced my first attempt.

Now, Imagine yourself in the room
as you continue reading...

The First Live Channelling

I am Kryon, of magnetic service. You are all so dearly loved. There are thirty eight entities here, some of which are in my service. It will take three minutes to get the room to the love vibration which I wish to project to you.

What is happening now is that we are clearing the floaters. I will explain floaters in a moment.

Each one of you is so dearly loved (*for I recognize your faithfulness in being in the right place when you should be, and I celebrate your willingness to participate in a window of opportunity for my partner*).

Thanks to my partner to giving credibility to the "nines," and while the energy is being supplanted (*my energy taking place of the existing energy here*), it is important that you understand the vibration of the "nine." Many of you already do, for it represents completion (*finish and conclusion, a wrap-up of events*) and it represents our time now. I'm sure that it has not been wasted on the mathematicians of Earth, or on some of you, that nine is the final, the highest of the single digits. It is appropriate to know that the nine multiplied by any number in the universe will equal an answer which adds to nine. There is no number which is higher, indicating again the completion. It is also no accident that where the meridians meet and the interlace takes place in the North and the South, that these have been deemed by the humans of long ago as 90 degrees North and 90 degrees South. (*Both are a nine vibration, for these are the poles of Earth, where my partner and I, plus two of you, helped anchor the interlace – the completion of the magnetic vortex at which the grids come to a grouped junction at both poles, and where humans appropriately should not ever try to live for any length of time).*

...And then finally *(it is)* for you to know that it is no accident that we come together on 3-3-1992 *(for this is a nine day, and was chosen by your group, not by the Kryon).*

The floaters in the room are gone. There are three balances *(of importance to the planet).* There is the balance of the entities on Earth, the balance of the vibrations and the balance of the magnetics. The entities have always been the same balance *(that is to say that the weight of spiritual entities on Earth has always remained constant. Do not confuse this with the vibration of the entities. You have no appropriate word or concept for this balance).* What has happened through the ages is that the floaters, the neutral entities, have been the placeholders. As the entities in lesson come in to the Earth plane, the floaters are displaced, and they leave. These *(floaters)* are the ones you have seen for years – the waifs, the gnomes, the little people. They are the floaters. *(They are neutral and cannot harm you. They represent only a place in the spiritual equation that holds a balance for the planet so that it retains consistent spiritual weight. They are also in lesson in their own right, and their interaction with you is to be minimal and not significant to your lesson. Many are visible to the enlightened, and can be a puzzle to many. Their vibration is so benign, however, that they are almost never feared.)*

There are no inappropriate entities here now. There are some very excited guides here, for I am Kryon. Please do not harden your hearts at this time. My message is not what my partner said it would be, for I am not here for validation. How many of you, when you enter a room filled with your loved ones, will spend much time proving that you are you? For I am Kryon, and I know you and you know me. I am the one you expected, and I bring wonderful news: incredible energy, and love and abundance for you.

Currently on Earth there are eight other entities channelling the Kryon. There are also many, many with the same message coming forth (the *message of the power you now have due to the shift I am creating*), but specifically you can look for eight *(representing the Kryon vibration)*. They are in the following places: Mexico, India, Africa, Russia, Israel, South America, China and Syria. In those areas they are specifically in the following places: Mexico, in the capital. India, in the new city. Africa, on the coast: 34 degrees South parallel, 18 degrees East meridian. In Russia, in Moscow... very powerful. In Israel, in the old city. In South America, 12 degrees South parallel, 77 degrees West meridian. In China and Syria – I will not disclose the locations.

I come before you tonight to give you the news, an admonition, some information... and love. *(The news is)* **The veil is lifting slightly**. *(This is the most significant change in the last 2,000 Earth years; you have only begun to recognize its meaning)*. I have asked my partner to write of this, and he has faithfully reproduced the information. With the lifting of the veil slightly, there is much that is going to come through.

Before we speak of that, those of you with perception and sight will know of my validation, even though you may doubt it now... for you will see the aura around my partner turn white. This is the neutralizing of his karmic attributes while I am channelling through him. *(This is only temporary, but is given while I am present to this degree to give my partner the power he needs to translate the thought energy as it arrives. You can use it as a measure of my presence any time you see him.)* The actual color of the Kryon entity is a deep copper, iridescent. This color may also superimpose itself on the white *(look for it to surround the aura)* while I am here.

As the veil lifts, you have the ability for so much power, as you have read *(for you)* to be able to leap over your karmic imprints... *(and)* to become powerful. The Earth needs you now!... in order for the transmutation of the energy *(of the negative to positive that will lift the planet to its final vibration and its appropriate consummation with the final lifting of the veil. I speak now specifically to the fourteen of you, for you are part of the many enlightened ones who will take the lead).*

Of the other two balances of the planet that I spoke of, one is vibration. The planet's vibration must be raised. You are to be congratulated that it is to what it is now *(being on schedule, and above what it was when I arrived).* But you must make it far higher. The balance will remain the same, even though the vibration increases. Like ice turns to water, then to steam, the matter remains the same, but the vibration will increase. *(The vibratory rate of anything, be it spiritual or physical, will not change the weight, only the energy consumption. In order for you to change the vibration of Earth, you will consume far more spiritual energy, which you may now receive directly from the singular love source. This is the key to why it is here! As the energy is consumed, the negativity becomes the waste product so to speak, and it is forever gone.)*

The admonition *(I spoke of earlier)* is as follows: As the veil cracks open, there will be many of you *(on Earth)* who will receive information. Please use collective discernment to tell truth from non-truth. It is as this: If someone came to Earth from another area of the universe, and they could spend five minutes here... and they came at night and stole into an Earth library with only a small light. *(Suppose)* they did not speak the language, but could look at the pictures. They looked at the books and left, *(and)* they went back to report *(to their leaders)*. What would they have seen *(that would lead them to draw conclusions about your planet)*? Would they have gathered pictures from your science fiction writers? Would they have gathered pictures of your history? Would they have grabbed books which had drawings that were meaningless... or perhaps your art... or perhaps they grabbed a sports almanac! What would they tell their people Earth was like? *(Can you imagine what they might conclude?)*

There is much of the same kind of thing *(now for you in comparison to the other side)* as the veil cracks open. There will be very vivid pictures of what things could be, but perhaps what they are not. You must use collective discernment to know the truth, what things really are. *(Do not hang on every concept that is presented to you. There could be much confusion now due mainly to the differences in the time frame on the two sides of the veil. Try to remember that our "now" is your past, present and future, just as in the library example. You might easily see thought energies projected that are only speculations of what will be. You already are aware that as humans you create thought energies about your future as an exercise to actually create it! There is much work on this side to prepare for your future as well, and in the process we prepare fully for all scenarios using the energy of thought. You may "tune in" to nothing more than a planning scheme, but the thought energies will land with much more clarity than before, and many will believe these things to be evident. Remember – no entity in the universe knows how you will do in the next years! If you receive supposed pictures of future events, weigh them in regards to what you really know to be the case. Stay in the love vibration, and bring yourselves together to decide, for you are more powerful and discerning when massed.)*

The love vibration in this room is starting to rise even further as some of you are understanding *(understanding that my real communication for you is in the Love vibration. Information is secondary and is given along the way. The real news is the power of the new energy... and I want you to feel it).* For you are so dearly loved! Your guides are here to serve you – not in judgment and they love you dearly. *(Your guides are the ones I really communicate with directly, for they have a direct line to the astral. I see them with you every time I see you. I never perceive you without them.)*

Another bit of information for you; this is important for you: **Celebrate the marking of time!** for you are in a linear time frame and we are not, speaking of those of you on the other side of the veil. Many of you understand right now what I am speaking of, for in this new energy you are going to be granted power. You will find abundance and you will find the peace that you desire. *(In the linear time frame one event must come before the other to accomplish your windows of opportunity like a train traveling along a track stopping at stations picking up the players and pieces of a puzzle. When the puzzle is complete, then your window can take place.)* But you have to wait at the station where the tracks are, because the train must pick up other things on the way to you. In your linear time frame this is the way these things are accomplished. *(This is addressed to those of you who are impatient with your windows of opportunity, especially for those of you who are enlightened. You have a real feeling for the "now" time frame that you know exists but cannot experience. You have difficulty waiting for the parts to come together to create what has been foretold, or promised for your life. This, then, is an admonition in love to be patient!)* The players must be picked up *(and assembled)* ... the things, the entities, the objects... and when they are ready, the train will come for you. This is when you get on. *(And not before! I know that you have tried to create your own windows of opportunity.*

This not only is inappropriate, it is dangerous, for in doing so, you actually might miss the real window!) You have the ticket in your hand, a promise. The tracks are in front of you. Why would you doubt this? *(Why would you doubt that the window is coming when you have been given a ticket by the universe, and you have stood here before and gotten on board?)* For it is coming! There is no doubt about it!

There are some who cannot even see the tracks, and they worry. *(You are different, however, for you understand the promise of the universe. There is much to be thankful for in this, for many are completely blind to the way things work, and have no concept that the window is coming. Know this: when you are in balance, everything works for the good of the whole: the whole body, mind and spirit. Abundance flows, health is good and peace is yours. You should be as a child with its parents, dressed up in wonderful clothing waiting at the train station for a trip to an exciting place. You are surrounded by those you love; you are abundant in the eyes of all. You have youth, and you are excited about where you are going. This analogy is perfect for the enlightened at this time. For if you find yourself anything less than this, then you need to examine your balance, and call on the love energy for healing.)* Celebrate the marking of time, for things must be in their place *(before your window can arrive).*

My partner is asking that I not push any harder than he is able to receive. *(I completely honor my partner's request at this time. This is appropriate for him to learn how to sublimate his ego, and will be significant in the future. Much will be learned from this sentence in the next months. Count on it.)*

There is so much love that I want to impart to each of you. I would like to hug each of you! For you are in service, even while you are in lesson, and there are not that many who are. *(This is why you are here tonight. You are the forerunners of the new energy, and by your example and your knowledge will you begin the transmutation work.)* We need action! and that is why I am here. For I am going to do my part, which is the third part of the balance *(the three balances of Earth that I communicated earlier).* As I align it and it moves *(the new magnetics),* it is appropriate that your power will increase. None of you tonight who have opened your heart to this message will go away unchanged. Some of you will have sleepless nights *(in the times to come).* This is because of the energy shift and the implants that I have *(prepared for you through your guides).* For many *(entities)* come to Earth right now for no other reason than to be your new guides... to adjust your implants and to celebrate the new energy, for you are deep within it already.

(Some of you here tonight are already perceiving the obvious difference during communication of the time frames between you and the Kryon. Many times I speak of the now, and it will be much "later" for you. I see things as happening all at once. Ever since I started this process with my partner, to me it has always been in the now, but to you it has occupied linear space along a path. I cannot expect you to suddenly grasp this concept, but here is a simple analogy: If you held in your hands one of your theatrical films, it would represent a chronology of linear time when viewed. While it is in your hand, however, all of the potential time is in your hand at once; it all is in the now. When you speak about what might happen at the 25 minute mark in the film, you don't have to wait 25 minutes to see it. For that portion of someone else's future is in your hand now, as well as the past. This is a description of how I see your path – not that I can see what is going to happen, as much as I see your windows of opportunity. If you are truly aware of this difference, then your understanding of these communications will be enhanced.)

I will entertain three questions that you will ask your guides collectively, and I will ask you to do that now, for my partner is not comfortable with the two-way interchange. I will take three of the collective questions. *(My partner must learn again not to fear failure, for in turning the questions over to me to choose, I will select the collective ones from all guides everywhere. This will service those reading this to come, but will not deal with those in attendance now. It is important to answer the questions from this group, which I will do at a later time through additional channelling and writing if my partner is willing.)*

The most asked question is about UFOs. There is another question about the **11:11**, and the third question is about the power spots on the magnetic grid.

There are two kinds of UFOs that you see and that you know about. It is easy to tell the difference between the two: One *(kind)* is from my side of the veil, and one is from yours. The kind from your side of the veil are easily photographed, with hard defined edges. They appear metallic. Of these kind from your side of the veil there are two categories: (1) the enlightened, and (2) the negative ones. Do not fear the negative ones, for you have power over them. They will also not be able to stay much longer because of the Earth's shift. My work will chase them away.

UFOs from the other side of the veil (the Kryon side) are not easily photographed, featuring soft edges. Most of them glow. They make occasional sounds. They appear to move very erratically as lights in the sky. This is because, again, they are not in a linear time frame as you are. They are in a real time frame. Just like your retrograde planets appear to move backwards when they are not, this is the same illusion... and the apparent motion is not what it is perceived to be. *(Planets in retrograde appear to move backwards because of the relativity of the platform you are traveling on in comparison to their motion. This is exactly what is happening with your time. The time differences create many illusions to you throughout the universe as you perceive it, but this UFO experience is the only case where you can watch it within your own magnetic field.)*

Of these *(kinds from my side)* there are many. One of the things that you do not realize is that what you are seeing is often not a UFO at all, but an actual entity. You assume because of your imprint and your implant that other entities are your human biological size, but they are not. My most comfortable size is about the size of one of your homes. That is the energy package as it is carried. This is the package you often "see." You are seeing entities instead of UFOs... instead of crafts *(you are seeing)* the actual spirit/soul entity. Sometimes we will clump together and come down, and you will see us separate. When we do this, the color of the whole will change. *(Each time one is added or subtracted, the larger will appear to change color.)*

Be aware: There are negative ones here from the other side of the veil *(my side)*. My admonition to you (and I will say no more on this subject at this time): In the new energy your power is no longer neutral. It is biased toward the positive therefore you have control over the negative entities... you have power and control over the negative entities... you have power and control over the negative entities. *(When the Kryon repeats three times, you know it is important. My dear ones, do not fear what you might perceive to be overwhelming negative force. These things are not for you to be concerned with, but since they occasionally are with you, I at least must give you instructions. Ignore them, and turn your back on them. Call on the singular love source and they will leave you alone. Do not be curious, for this allows them to interact with your lesson, and it is inappropriate that this take place.)*

Do not be alarmed at the increase in activity of the UFOs. We have many coming from many places. There is constant, continual travel between here and my support group in the orbit of Jupiter. There are many coming from all over to celebrate this time... with your help. *(Most of the activity is centered around the service of each of you as a human, ready to receive new spiritual gifts and guides. It is almost as a changing of the guard is to a palace, for those who have serviced you in the past energy now leave to make new paths, and are replaced by those ready to take up the task in the new energy. Be aware that there is much excitement about the change! What is happening here does not always occur, and there is celebration for your experiences to come.)*

Both kinds of UFOs *(your side and mine)* use the magnetic grid, ironically, for their travel. Even the entities coming into the atmosphere will tend to travel on the grid. With the realignment of the grid, the landing places will change. *(In a private communication with your teacher Barbra, I spoke of the fact that the train can only go where the tracks are... in reference to the activities of UFO landing locations. There is much to glean from this knowledge alone. If you ask the right questions, and draw the obvious conclusions, you will learn much about the way magnetics are used as a power source.)*

The next question we have is about the grid and the power spots. You might find it interesting to know that part of your power is stored on the grid, and it always has been. This is what you "feel" in the power spots where you travel, for you have not always been able to contain all of your own power. *(There is much to teach on this subject, but it is only interesting, and does nothing at this time to get on with the task at hand. For those who are interested, the "piece of God" that your soul entity represents here on Earth has retained every bit of universal energy that it had while on the other side of the veil. Much of the energy is stored, however, in several collective places, and not within your body. This is appropriate, for otherwise you would have no lessons! The grid is the medium that allows for much of the storage, but there is also some storage deep within the Earth where a portion of the "engine" for the grid is placed. This is complex, and isn't necessary for your path at this time.)*

(The chronology of energy available for your soul is fascinating, however, even to me for it directly involved the great masters of your past, and brought me here to you now. Jesus came to tell you that you finally had the ability to contain it, and now I come to facilitate it!) It is only with the opening of this window *(the new energy)* that allows you to finally take your power and do the things you've only dreamed of. *(This is in regard to the voiding of your implants that have kept you in lesson, and have hindered you from attaining full enlightenment.)* As that happens, you will draw from the power spots. What used to be power spots will then be neutral. They are storage areas for you. This is part of the balance *(I spoke of earlier)*, for the energy of the Earth has always remained the same. It only flows between things, *(in this case)* between the grid and your souls in lesson. *(Therefore, eventually there will be no more "power spots" for you to live within, or travel to, and feel better.)* So to answer the question "where to move?" which has been asked tonight, wherever it feels good now, may not later. If you want some advice: if you can, your best work will be done where it is cool.

Finally a question about the 11:11. What is it? This should be obvious. It is the gateway. It represents this period of time for eleven years. It represents the Kryon energy, for I did not come here out of my own choosing. There is a plan and a direction that was predestined that I arrive. My partner did not make up my name. The name Kryon in your language was suited because it is the eleven vibration *(represented by English letters added in the fashion I specified in the earlier writing, which is the easiest for those untrained in numbers).* Not only that, but it contains portions of the sound tone quality which will also be contained in the eight other Kryon channellers on the Earth. Look for the "iiiieeaaahh" in any of those names, finishing off not with a consonant *(sudden stop),* but with an "nnnnnnn" or an "uummmm." That is the Kryon. Those of you who have read the material *(the Kryon communications as written by my partner up to this date),* and have done any of the numbers and added them together, will understand and realize that I arrived 1-1-1-9-8-9. This is eleven. My departure 1-2-3-1-2-0-0-2, is eleven. *(These are dates of arrival and departure that I gave your partner, that have been presented for your study through the writings to this date. There is much to be gleaned from the observation of the number meanings within the writings. If you compute the beginning of the new energy from 1/1/1992 to 12/31/2002, you will also realize that I will be with you in the new energy exactly eleven years.)* This is part of the 11:11 window. It was foretold by the ancients. It is the power change. This is your gift that you have earned at this point in time. There is very little you cannot do with your new power, but it must start with yourselves *(as I have already given direction)* and with CHOICE!

In other channellings, I will tell you about healing, for there are those in this room right now who need it. There is an adrenal problem... healing could be instant. There is anxiety... someone is worried about... their car. These things *(speaking about the trivial)* you must lift yourselves beyond, for the love energy is so far above any of these. These things do not deserve your attention.

Before I leave I would like you to see me. You will finally have some insight as to how the colors and patterns are put together for any entity. And again, if you will follow my direction, I would like to take you very briefly up and beyond the Earth's atmosphere. Those of you who have had "out of body" experiences in the past, which my partner never has, will know this is accurate. I would like to have each of you open your hearts and allow for this.

If you would imagine in your mind that you are now floating above the clouds. You are above the atmosphere of the Earth and it is very dark. Your energy has expanded to its full size. And now as you look beneath you, you will see something that's different, *(something that is)* indicative of the new energy. For those of you who have done this before will realize that there is something missing: the silver tether is gone! This is your permission to keep going if you choose. (but none of you will). You are free, and as you approach me, I will be still. Feel the love vibration around me... for I love you so dearly! It is of singular origin. It is the universal love. It vibrates so fast that it cannot be seen. *(Therefore it represents incredible power and energy from a source that appears black.)*

As you behold me, you will see that I have eleven sides, and that each side is a pattern. *(Please note that the patterns are not symmetrical, and that none are alike.)* Like a stained-glass window, it is segmented. Each side has a color of its own. As you approach and circle me, I will start to spin. As I spin up to the vibration which is the Kryon energy, you will see my color take place that is the Kryon energy. For it is a total culmination of the eleven sides spinning together, blending as one. What you *(are able to)* perceive is only a fraction, a residue of the true vibration, for most of it is out of your range *(of human sight)*. What is left is a beautiful iridescent copper color. This is the Kryon color *(for you)*. The other entities which will come to you in the future during these *(new energy)* years will be of dark blues and dark greens, and many other beautiful darker colors. These *(perceived colors)* are simply the residue left from what you <u>cannot see</u>. This is why the colors are darker than you expect. *(You have always seen us with lower vibratory rates before this time due partially to the types of entities serving you in the last 2,000 years. These lower rates ironically seemed to be far more colorful and intense because they were more in your sight range.)* As I spin up to full speed, you can see the glory of this entity, and realize that each of you looks just like this, with different colors, slightly different sizes, and many different patterns.

As we all spin together, you can feel the love I have for you. *(This is a state I would like to bring you into any time we are together in the future. Much information can be communicated this way, and the love source can really be effective for you. You have no idea what can be accomplished for you personally if you can obtain this state with me.)*

Now as you come back down, I admonish you to put the small things away, for there is work to be done. *(The small things that I speak of are those of which you ponder now, like direction for yourselves and how to go about life. By putting them away, I mean that you must completely trust that these things will be shown to you at the appropriate time, and that you must not let them occupy your main energy now. For you have so much more to do for the planet, and that is the important task. You have contracts to do this! Your higher-self knows this, and your intuition will be heightened to allow for your conscious mind to also know, so you can take solace, and have peace with this knowledge.)*

I AM Kryon, and you are dearly loved.

With this, I have fulfilled my obligation for the live channelling.

The writer.

Chapter Four

Answers

Kryon Answers
Chapter Four

Kryon responds to specific questions

Almost to the day, ninety days later, the Metaphysical group of fourteen respond to the live channel with a group of seven questions. I will include all questions and answers, even though some of them may be time specific to the early nineties when this communication was given. Here are the questions that the Metaphysicians asked:

1. Are you aware of the Hopi land map and, if so, how do you view it?

2. Will it be necessary for large numbers of humankind to be terminated in order to achieve balance on planet Earth?

3. Will the indigo children be in time to accomplish at least most of what they have come to do?

4. How long do you think it will take for the meridian line adjustments?

5. What is the main point for individuals personally to focus on for day-to-day living?

6. Besides working on myself personally, what can I do to make a difference in the world for humanity?

7. Can you describe a physical exercise for centering for better alignment in receiving information?

As you look at these questions, do you understand the language? If not, perhaps the answers given will help you understand the context. These are obviously very well thought out questions of vital interest to those who are enlightened. It may serve you to find out more about the subjects being asked about. You have to wonder: if these people want to know about them, then maybe you should too?

The questions will be answered literally, and specifically for those who asked them as individuals living in the Southern California area of the United States. In this respect they may not be as general as other writings in the book. As in the past this foreword is being written prior to the channel, and I do not know at this moment what the answers will be. Find out with me as you continue to read...

New Answers For New Times

In perfect love I again greet you! I am aware of all the questions, and I am once again so very pleased that they show how much you really understand about your time in this new energy.

It is vitally important that this translation be clear! I will ask my partner to again clear his mind of all else but what is at hand. The first two questions will be taken as one. They are the following:

Question: Are you aware of the Hopi land map, and if so, how do you view it?

Question: Will it be necessary for large numbers of humankind to be terminated in order to achieve balance on planet Earth?

Answer: These questions relate to each other (as you will see), and are questions based in fear. This is not a criticism, only a fact. Dear ones, I will answer these, for you deserve it. But I will also set the stage so that you can understand more fully why you choose to know these things (for you might find it interesting), and why the answer is the way it is.

Almost without exception, those who were present for my partner's first live channel have something in common: you all have an underlying biological fear of being crushed or drowned at the hands of a natural Earth disaster.

Fear of termination while in lesson is absolutely natural, but there is more than this basic feeling with the fourteen of you. Remember that I know who you are, and I know your past expressions. All of you were present in ancient Atlantis, and each of you in some way feels you were betrayed by the Earth at that time. To some of you this may seem fantastic, but please read on.

Although all of you were terminated by contract (*prior agreement with a plan set in motion by yourself and the universe*), you have carried the "seed feelings" of that termination with you all this time. Seed feelings are those emotions you carry with you as part of your imprint through many expressions. This is not the appropriate time to reveal the past workings of your karmic group, or why Atlantis was terminated. But remember in a past message I said that I had been here before? ...and that the last two times humanity was terminated so that I could make my adjustments? (*page 21 of this book*) Well, here I am again making adjustments! Is it no wonder that you feel anxious? For the last time you felt my entity, I helped create your termination! As described earlier in the writings, each of you knows me. The God part of you recognizes and celebrates the God part of me. Although you all have full knowledge of how we interrelate, right now (*because you are in lesson*) you appropriately are only allowed to peek through a dim glass at me, and to remember only the most intense seed feelings when you saw me last. I love you dearly. Please do not fear me; I am not here for another planetary termination.

Both of these questions have to do with mass termination of humanity, for the prophecy map of Hopi origin speaks its silent message of mass destruction within the new smaller outlines of the land masses. Will the Earth betray you again (you might ask)?

My answer to this question will be highly logical, for the universe is thus. I will prepare by giving you some facts. These facts are both from my previous writings thus far, and from new thoughts as well. All facts, if understood, will lead you to the correct enlightened answer when I complete the exercise.

I am Kryon, the magnetic master. My work gives me tremendous insight into the human biological psyche, since my magnetic adjustments are interrelated to the workings of your consciousness while on Earth (*pages 19 & 20*). I also have knowledge of your past and your future windows of opportunity. These are windows you may or may not walk through, not windows of predestination. Your questions regarding the Earth and termination of humanity are dripping with hidden truth. It's time you realized the significance of the Earth connection. This will help you in realizing the answer to your own questions.

The Earth Partnership

It is deep rooted in your western culture that the Earth is separate and apart from the biological and spiritual human individual. When a person is seen as non spiritual in your culture they are said to be "earthly" or "worldly." This sets up a negative partnership which not only shows how little humans in your culture understand things, but also gives negative verbalization to something very, very sacred.

Let me ask you the following questions for you to answer in your mind: Based on my teachings so far: (1) When the Kryon entity arrived over and over for your planet, what work was accomplished? (2) When doing the work, what part of the planet did the Kryon specifically address? (3) What was the end result of the work?

The answers are: (1) The work accomplished was to alter the magnetic alignment of the **Earth**. (2) The specific parts addressed were the magnetic grids of **Earth**. and (3) The end result of the work was to provide enlightenment for **humans**. At this point you might ask yourself: if the end result was for humans, then why would the Kryon address the physical Earth? Why not address humans directly? The answer to that, dear ones, is that I did – by addressing the Earth! Most of the fourteen of you know exactly of what I speak, but for others reading this now, I will elaborate as I deal with your questions.

The Earth and the human in lesson are an inseparable partnership. You cannot be balanced unless you understand your root partnership with the planet, through your connection with the heart of the Earth. This is a spiritual connection, and was with you from the beginning of time when it was set up for you. Your specific culture chose to separate themselves from the Earth, not realizing that to do so would also separate humans from tremendous power, enlightenment and balance. You must treat the Earth as a live, on-going partner, and celebrate its existence, and honor its health. The Earth not only gives you food and protection, it gives you your seed consciousness, provides for enlightenment (through the alignment of the grids), allows for protection from disease, regularly balances and heals itself (with no help from you) and is the actual parent of your base biology. In addition, it stands by with unlimited resources and power that you have not recognized yet! Added to this is the army of entities within the Earth that is there with universal correctness to help balance the life force on the planet.

Why do I tell you this? So you will have an appreciation of the cultures that do indeed celebrate the Earth... for these cultures are the very ones that are on the leading edge of enlightenment. And these are the cultures that entities like the Kryon have been dealing with directly for many, many years. ,

Who are they? They represent cultures all over the globe, specifically South America, India, Asia, Australia and the remaining culture you call the American Indian Nation. Many of you will recognize immediately that these are often the focal point of much UFO activity, and as I stated during my partner's direct channel with you (*pages 82-84*), many of the UFOs originate from my side of the veil. Therefore, I am giving you a truth: there is much spiritual communication going on from my side with these groups, more so than with those of your culture.

With this in mind I will tell you that the Hopi map* was channelled at the highest source, and had the potential to be entirely accurate. You should also know, however, that the information on the Hopi map (and the "*I am America*" map) is not new at all. This information has been available for well over 400 years. The most famous to write it was a European in the 16th century. His map and the Hopi map are very similar, except that his map has your houses under water within the next few years. The Hopi map has your houses sitting on one of the only surviving areas! So which is true? Also early Hopi knowledge had an entirely different cause for the new outline of the land, and as your human

*For the "I am America" map, write PO box 2511, Payson, AZ 85547

history changed, new updated reasons and causes were given for the same prophecy. Why did that change?

I give you these different interpretations to again tell you: **not one entity in the universe can predict the actual outcome of your on-coming test!** (*page 24*) Knowing full well that you would ask these items, I also admonished you within your own live channel with my partner about this very thing when I spoke of receiving vivid pictures from my side of the veil of what things <u>might be</u>. Please read this again, for it will now mean more than it did when you originally heard it (*pages 77,78*). This Hopi prophecy information has come accurately, representing the probable outcome of the planet **based on the consciousness and enlightenment at the moment of the channel**. Why do you think that 400 years ago your city was prophesied as sinking, and the Hopi prophecy provides for its safety? What changed? The answer is that you changed your city! There can be no greater example of my point. Your work on the planet can change these predictions. The love source is able to do it through you. Therefore do you understand the future is not set? There is more logical information to give you about your area, and I will give it at the end of this section before dealing with more questions.

More on the Hopi map: The five power spots fully agree with my planned realignment for your continent. This is important: It is not necessary for the new land outline of the continent to be accomplished for the new power spots to be accurate. These power areas are actually ports from which the engine within the Earth can be applied to the grid system. This is complex, and is not necessary information for your growth at this time. Although the geography describing the ports is accurate, my admonishment isn't to go there to live. If this were true, I would have advised you of it at the very beginning. Remember you are pieces of God. It is not necessary to pull your power from anywhere but what you already have within yourself. Those who do not understand this will be attracted to go live in those areas.

Finally on the subject of the Earth partnership, I must tell you that regardless of your new implants, and regardless of how peaceful you have become, and regardless of your level of enlightenment, you absolutely will react to the stress of the Earth. This is exactly why you must work to raise the vibratory level of the actual physical planet. The planet is your partner, and it is alive with you. Many of you are responsive to geological activity, whether it be volcanic, seismic, aquatic, magnetic, or geothermal. If you feel the stress of the Earth, then you are indeed tuned in to the partnership. This is normal, and isn't something that is going to change for you. The way to change it is to change the planet. Now do you understand why I am able to change <u>you</u> by changing the magnetics of the <u>physical</u> planet? This is science in its purest form: the marriage of the physical to the spiritual.

As for the second question about mass termination: Will it be necessary for large numbers of humankind to be terminated in order to achieve balance? The answer is yes. The numbers, however, only approach one percent of the life force here. This is not a global termination (as I promised you earlier). Who will it be?

It is thus: those with absolutely no hope whatsoever of achieving any greater enlightenment than they already have will move on. This is also complex, and has to do with karmic groups and star karma. It has already begun. My former writings spoke of these things when I gave you information about governments making decisions for the masses (*page 26*). Your Gulf war was a prime example of how tens of thousands left the planet together in a few days. Other wars, some involving tribe against tribe, will do the same. Another example is starvation. Basically through the non-action of other humans, an entire karmic grouping will actually starve, and leave the planet together. Many will also leave through the new disease, especially in Africa. The other way is through unusual natural events. By unusual I mean events that are not predictable or expected.

Regarding the area you live in: do not necessarily associate your Earthquake threat with the end times. What you have facing you is simple geology, and a very localized situation at that. Of course any major natural quake is universally appropriate, as well as the appropriate termination of life that occurs with it. It may seem catastrophic to you when it occurs, just like it did to the Asians during theirs, or the South Americans during theirs, but it is not a global event. You have known of this moving area for over 100 years in your country. For 30 years you have known exactly what causes it and where it might happen. You continue to live in the area anyway, even with the knowledge that eventually the Earth will move on a given plane, and probably cause you hardship. I have told you of your partnership with the Earth. Can you imagine the effect on you to live in an area where the ground is always stressed? If the plants and animals can tell (and they can), then you should also realize that your balance is disturbed by this.

During your live channel session I advised you to move to where it was cool. This was literal advice, for the Kryon has no motives other than to provide you with good information that will allow peace in your life right now. If you are worried about your area, and the many predictions of geological activity coming up... then you should not stay. Move north to where it is cooler, or east where it is cooler. These are the best areas for you. In general it is logical and practical never to allow yourself to remain in a situation that makes you anxious. Isn't this simple knowledge for you? Surely it does not take my wisdom to advise you on this.

Before I continue with the other questions, I wish to again give you the advice that if you are not comfortable with the ancient predictions, then you should leave. Others will have group discernment that will enable them to have peace with the non-appropriate predictions. You will see many "doom and gloom" predictions pass by with nothing happening at the appointed "worry time." Some of you will have to go through these to fully believe what I am saying here. I have come here to give you love, power, energy and enlightenment – because you have earned it. Do not stress yourself on the "what if" factor during your lesson. Your entire human biology is primed at this time to move forward in concert with my work. Do not spend time generating thought energy around things that might never take place. This will not serve you! Please continue to read as I answer questions that may help you have peace over your concerns.

Question: Will the indigo children be in time to accomplish at least most of what they have come to do?

Answer: You may recall that I gave information regarding the new age auric colors, specifically the new dark blues that are coming in at this time (*page 61*). These are what you are undoubtedly calling the "indigo" children, for at this particular stage every human with this condition is a child. (*Kryon Book six has more information on the "indigo" children.*)

Your question would lead me to believe that you consider this group to have special purpose. This is not the case. Let me explain: These individuals are simply new expressions that have the equipment that you did not, namely that of, (1) higher vibration, (2) an imprint that voids certain astrological attributes that usually affect all humans, and (3) specific biological equipment to enable them to better handle the human manufactured impurities of the planet that are now part of the human way of life. These individuals come in as a new breed of expression, having inherited what you have helped create (an altered imprint). Those of the planet who leave during this time (and there will be many, as indicated by the last questions) will be able to return immediately in this new condition (if appropriate), thereby helping the planet in the new age of power. It isn't guaranteed that these individuals will necessarily be any more enlightened than others, or that they will band together as a group to accomplish specific planetary tasks.

As they mature, however, some will be able to cut through the normally difficult human transitions to full enlightenment, and at a very early age they will be able to help with the tasks of raising the planet's vibration along with all of you. There are two very obvious secrets hiding in what I have just given you, and one of them answers your question directly.

(1) The reason why so many must leave the planet at this time is to allow for them to return as indigo children! Do you see how powerful this will be for the planet's transition? (2) If they are only now beginning to come in with the new equipment, then you already know a secret about the future! Naturally you know how long it takes for a human to mature. Do your arithmetic on this. Does it seem as though you might be able to work a full 20 years or more? The answer is yes. This revealed secret gives you a projected time frame which might be different than you expected. It is our prediction **based on the consciousness and enlightenment at the moment of this channel**. Yes there will be time. Do you wish to know how much time? Then read the next answer.

Question: How long do you think it will take for the meridian line adjustments?

Answer: Literally answered: just as long as for the parallel ones! (*cosmic humor*) The intent of your question I believe is to ask how long the grid adjustments will take. I depart on 12/31/2002 (*page 86*). All adjustments will be in place by this date. This answer, as the last one, should give you a more comfortable feeling about the length of time you have to accomplish your task. You will have at least 10 to 15 years after I leave to work within my finalized adjustments. You have earned this.

Read This!

My partner wishes me to make this information very clear, for it is obvious that many of you do not yet understand the significance of all of this:

1. Your millennium is coming to an end.

2. It was prophesied in many cases that this would also be the end of all life on Earth, for a termination was in order, and the school was going to be turned into a neutral place for yet another school. The preparation time for the new school would have been another 1,000 years; and yes, I would be returning yet again to realign after that.

3. **This has now been changed!** You will not be terminated. You will not necessarily go through horrible wars and planetary upheaval that would have culminated in you leaving by the year 2001. You have earned the right to stay and control your own destiny completely, <u>well into the first century of the new millennium</u>. This you have done yourselves by raising the vibration of the planet through thought consciousness over the last 60 years (at the eleventh hour, you might say).

4. As described so far in these writings, many will terminate and return with new powers. Also the transition to this new age of self determination and power will be filled with changes. Things will not remain the same for any of you, but I have given you news that should make the changes far easier.

Now you have the knowledge of exactly what is happening, and I am telling you that you have far more power to "ride with it" than you ever did before. Have peace over these things! Believe me, if you cannot have peace during this time, then you will not stay. The years you have put in working with the universe so far should have made you wiser, not so staid in your ways that you cannot accept universal appropriate change. Dear ones, these are your times; take them!

Question: What is the main point for individuals personally to focus on for day-to-day living?

Answer: This question and the next two are about doing the work. This is why you are celebrated so! You didn't only ask about the danger; you really do want to work! I expected nothing less. Consider this question and the next two as a group of three to be used together for yourself. The first question deals with your spiritual health from day to day. The second question (to follow) deals with your work for humanity, and the third question (to follow) deals with the procedure to accomplish both.

I will answer this first question literally. You have to deal with what's wrong in your day-to-day life before you can expect to move on to higher things. The main point for you to focus on from day to day is to regain the peace and balance that is suppose to accompany your enlightenment. To allow for this, my first admonition is to stop creating your own negative vortices! Your day-to-day living is packed with non-appropriate reactions to events and other humans. How can you do the work when your thoughts are preoccupied by emotions caused by these things? All my teachings so far in this book deal with changing your imprint through accepting new implants to let you do this. Do you see the correlation now? My grid alignments are being calibrated to reinforce this change in you, and to give you more power to accomplish it. These things are all part of your new abilities.

You have to concentrate day to day on not reacting to the "buttons" that you have allowed to be pushed in your minds all these years. Did another human cause you insult or pain? Did something apparently go incorrectly? Did a person disappoint you? On a day-to-day basis, get control of these things. You can almost totally void them! When you do, you will know it. Believe me, you will feel different. The third question's answer will help you with the method. This is the goal: bring peace into your lives so that you can do the work. When you learn to control your response to previously anxious items, you gain power. This power lifts you to a place that allows you to do it again and again. Finally you will also understand that the events around you that seemingly are not in your control are actually very much in your control.

It is essential that you learn to recognize these day-to-day things as they happen so that you can void them one by one. It is also essential that you learn to see the truth within yourselves about how you have been treating these anxieties. Some humans are so accustomed to living with these vortices, that to be without them actually creates anxiety and unrest! Peace is a natural state, and yet some of you tend to create your own negative vortices, and wallow in them so others will give you attention. When you are balanced, your guides will give you all the attention you ever wanted.

This is probably not the answer you expected from this question, and yet it is the appropriate one. You have asked how to clean the inside of the jar, and I have answered that first you must get control of the lid in order to open it.

Question: Besides working on myself personally, what can I do to make a difference in the world for humanity?

Answer: This question has many facets. For now I will cover only the essentials. You have to start with the Earth itself in order to help humanity. You simply can't raise the vibratory rate of enlightenment for the planet unless you address the issue of the physical Earth first. After that you can concentrate on spiritual matters of the human race. The partnership with the Earth I spoke of is critical to allowing for your own growth.

(1) Physical: In order of importance you must first insist as inhabitants of the Earth that you dedicate your knowledge and science to stop the attrition of Earth's important self-balancing resources. This subject has many parts, but the most important one right now is the planet's atmosphere. Get control over the depletion of the chemicals in the upper layers. You don't yet realize how important this is. If you do not control this first, then your weather will change. When your weather changes, your areas for growing food for the population will change, and many will starve in places that you would never expect. This is paramount!

Next you __must__ get rid of your artificially produced, volatile small particle fuels. These are absolutely the most dangerous substances on Earth. Use your science and start a discovery program to neutralize these deadly materials. If you start now, by 1999 you will receive a scientific window of opportunity that will reward you with results. Abandon the use of these materials for any purpose whatsoever. As a race of intelligent beings, why would you ever have developed and manufactured a poison that you could not control, and barely contain, in such mass quantity? Begin using your enlightened minds to understand the two important inexhaustible areas where power for your cities should be drawn from: (1) There is unlimited heat directly below the feet of every human on Earth. And you already understand that heat equals power. It should never be necessary to consume anything for heat. Learn how to obtain and harness it! (2) Understand the incredible consistent energy of the tidal actions on your coasts. (After all, isn't that where many of your major cities are?) The universe has provided you with tons and tons of push-pull action – just waiting for you to use it! You already understand the benefits of hydro-electric power. It's yours; it's free, clean, and it's forever.

The nations of the Earth are already starting to address these problems, and you can watch what will happen: First it will bring the cultures together. This is a promoter of peace. Peace is a catalyst for the vibration raising of any planet. Without human energy and resources being expended on war and war planning, there is less and less thought energy going into destroying others. These planning sessions also create tolerance between nations, a prime ingredient for beginning enlightenment. All these things help <u>void negativity</u>. This, therefore, is one method of the transmutation process I have spoken of. In addition to all this, you will be amazed at how your war economies can be changed into environmental economies. The more humans employed in any way with the work of helping the planet, the more rewards in abundance for the workers. Your culture is driven by this, and I as Kryon have understanding of these things, for I have seen it many times. If you wish your nation to be the leader nation in the next 11 years, then invest your efforts now while you can in environmental invention and discovery; otherwise you will find yourself working for the others. Your science is ripe now for good discoveries in important environmental areas. We will help you, but you must start.

(2) Spiritual: Assemble together and provide positive thought energy for the planet and the human race. There is much new hidden power in this process, but the procedure must be understood and implemented correctly. In the new energy you can create a great deal more than the sum of the whole. That is, if a group of enlightened people are aligned and balanced, and are in touch with the guides, their combined energy creates a power exponent which is the quotient of one third their number.

(*Example: A group of twelve would create an exponent of 4: twelve people divided by three, equals four. Therefore the exponent would be twelve to the fourth power, or 20,736!*) You can see that a nominal number of enlightened persons can create the power of a stadium filled with good intentional non-enlightened persons. This is new. You never had anything like this kind of power before, but you must understand how to proceed. With this in mind, can you see how the few can effect the many?

Question: Can you describe a physical exercise for centering for better alignment in receiving information?

Answer: It is not by chance that the procedure to align for better reception is the identical procedure for transmission of thought energy. In the last answer I spoke of how important it was to understand and implement this process correctly. I cannot stress this enough. It will be a science! The results will be so astounding that you will constantly be searching for more refined methods. What I will give you here are the beginning basics. More will come later. This answer really has two parts: (1) for a group and (2) for an individual. This is not as much a physical exercise as a procedure. No single exercise will bring you anything close to what follows.

For both procedures I must stress that these instructions are literal and concise, and there is much more to be explained in detail about each step. I have given my partner information on this, and if appropriate, he can further inform you if you desire it.

The prime ingredients are (**A**) self preparation (**B**) guide communication (**C**) information reception and/or transmission. The most important new power rests in the second. Your guides are your key to both reception and transmission. You can't have communication with the universe without them. This is their sole purpose. As described earlier in the writings, your full God entity is carried with you, but you cannot get to it except through the guides (*pages 52-54*).

For a group: First, come to do the work. An unbalanced person in the group can drastically affect the power. Decide together the subject of what you are going to create as your target. Be careful that your subject and your target are universally appropriate. With the amount of power you now wield, you have great responsibility in this. Establish a team leader to move you collectively through the steps. Only concentrate on one task at a time; diluting it with multiple tasks will dilute the result. Do not let detractors even get close to this gathering.

A: self preparation

(1) Use what you already know and understand about body orientation and posture to align yourselves together in your group. This is not new information, and it has not changed. A north/south and/or east/west orientation will be helpful, but isn't critical. (*In other words try to square yourself up with the magnetic grid, but you can face each other. Use a compass for this.*) Be certain you are away from magnetic interference.

(2) Use a strong visualization to put away all thoughts that are not in universal love. If you feel unbalanced in any way, then excuse yourself from the group. It will hurt the efforts of the whole.

(3) Spend time in self realization. Understand that you are a piece of God, veiled in form, walking on Earth. Visualize yourself as the entity you are. Love yourself. Understand the meaning of the "I AM."

(4) Call on the love source to fill you with peace. It has to come when called. It is your right. "See" your favorite personal ascended master if it will help to bring in the love.

(5) Visualize yourself as an extension of those around you. Count the numbers around you and "see" them with you as a single, whole entity. See your face on each of their bodies. Feel their love for you.

(6) Allow your ego to void itself. Understand how temporary is the expression you are now, compared to who you really are when not on Earth.

B. Guide communication

(1) Acknowledge your guides presence verbally **out loud**. Do this individually, but audibly. Tell the guides that you love them and honor them for their work with you. Feel their love. Ask for them to touch you. Weep within the joy if you feel inclined to, for it is natural and appropriate to do so.

This last step is critical. Without it your work is useless. Understand the role of the guides, and there is nothing you cannot create! These are your conduits to the other side of the veil. You won't be able to communicate unless you understand this.

(2) With the team leader in control, explain briefly to the guides about the project at hand, and what the target is. Do not assume that the guides know anything of what you are doing. Guides are consistently astral, and are never in your cultural consciousness. Always be very literal in the explanation, and be careful to only give them the information as to the end target result, and not instructions on how to accomplish it.

(3) Together ask the guides to join you.

(4) Be silent and meditative. Allow time for transition. Visualize how powerful you now have become.

B. The work

You may accomplish either (1) transmission, or (2) reception, or (3) both. At this point all can occur, but the following is specifically for transmission. *(Reception, however, will always follow to some degree during this time.)*

(1) Let the team leader verbally describe and provide a strong visualization of the target action. This should be in the form of seeing the task accomplished, not how it is to be accomplished. In other words, see the end result as though you had been totally successful in the first moments of your work.

(2) With the team leader assisting, provide a unison verbalization (out loud) of the <u>end result</u>.

This is not a request of the universe at this point! This is a generated thought action meant to <u>create</u> a final result. You must understand that you are <u>creating</u> now, <u>not asking</u>. The team leader may prepare in advance the specific language of these verbalizations, so that they are proper and appropriate. Be very careful to visualize exactly what you want, for that is what will take place. As a beginning, visualize your planet as stable. Visualize your planet in physical peace, without external cataclysm ever touching it. Visualize your planet in harmony with the entities that reside on and in it. Visualize and verbalize your planet as balanced!

Only after you have dealt with the physical Earth should you begin to deal with visualizations regarding other humans. This is the appropriate priority, and should tell you much of how your spirituality for the future is to be determined.

(3) Do this a total of three times. Whatever is your verbal cycle, do it three times. This is not a time to be timid. Feel that what you are doing is of the utmost importance. Speak slowly and with conviction and peace. Realize your power. Do this as you would order it done.

(4) Note the time it has taken for you to do steps one through three, and provide that same amount of time in total silence and meditation. This is where you will receive information, or simply receive love energy. Do not feel it would be inappropriate to express quiet inward emotion at this time in the meeting. Provide whatever outside physical sense stimulation will help enhance this (*music, smells, lighting, etc.*).

(5) With the leader in control, return gradually to the state where you started.

This process should not last longer than one hour of your time. The identical meeting with the same target should be repeated again to allow for other universal alignments to do their work. If you are balanced, the small planet retrogrades should not interfere in this communication. But the larger planetary aspects will, so repeat it.

Personally, all of you can obtain the same kind of individual communication and centering with these steps. In fact it is necessary for you to do this in order to have your lives peaceful and abundant. Again use the same prime ingredients: (**A**) self preparation, (**B**) guide communication, (**C**) information reception and transmission. Verbalize everything! Communicate clearly the end result of what you desire to your guides, and you will have it. Use the same rules and principles contained in the aforementioned lists, but obviously without team leadership.

I have asked my partner to write more about your personal communication with your guides from a human perspective at the end of this book, for he is being given experience in this. This is what makes these writings different and special to many of you. I am Kryon of magnetic service, speaking through a human of limited Metaphysical service. This partnership brings you a simple book with practically written truths. Granted there is much, much more to how the universe works, but for now you need to understand the basics of the new energy written in this manner. (Please see chapter seven.)

I have answered the seven questions put forward by the group of fourteen. These questions were all very appropriate for your times, and the answers should be examined by all, not just those who asked them. It is never my intention to be vague or veiled in my instructions to you. If any-  thing here has seemed so, please remember that your future is not set. Answers cannot be given to what might happen, but instructions can be given for you to create what will happen. Realize your power, and create your future accordingly.

You all are dearly loved!

Kryon

On The Internet!
http://www.kryonqtly.com

California site

Internet Address
http://www.kryon.com

This is the California Kryon web site. See the daily updated Kryon seminar schedule. See the latest channels (including all the United Nations transcriptions). See what Kryon products are available, and read the latest Kryon book reviews. Subscribe to the Kryon Quarterly Magazine. This is the Kryon "commercial" area. (Both Kryon sites are available from [www.kryonqtly.com].

On The Internet!
http://www.kryonqtly.com

Florida site

Internet Address
http://www.kryon.org.

This is the Florida Kryon web site. Receive "marshmallow messages," personally chosen and sent to your EMAIL each day. Join in a chat room with others of like mind. Spend time on the message board. Find others in your area of the same consciousness. This is the Kryon "family" area - warm and toasty! (Both Kryon sites are available from [www.kryonqtly.com].

"I am Kryon in service to you in lesson.
You are the exalted ones.
You are the ones who have chosen to
come in and die repeatedly for the
benefit of your planet and the universal
plan of things. For this, we have honored
you with respect, and love without
measure".

Chapter Five

Healing and Disease

Healing and Disease
Chapter Five

The Beginning of Transmutation Teaching

I t is not within universal correctness that I as Kryon would give to you answers to questions of which have not seen their appropriate window for presen-tation. This is to say that as students you can see the wisdom of your teacher not simply giving the answers to tests, but rather mak-ing you learn the lessons, and then working out the answers for yourself. You approach this in the same way for your young on Earth.

However, I know you also understand that all inventions, discoveries of nature, and even things so apparently random as finding old historical civilizations, are all "given" by the universe. I'm certain that you all have noticed that science information is often presented to you in the form of enlightenment and discovery at many points of the planet at once. This is to say that although it may seem that one human came up with an idea, it was given to many. And the one who received the credit was the one who honored the intuition of the presentation the fastest, and put the information together with known past information to create new science. Please note that the beginning of all scientific information is the spiritual presentation of the ideas at the appropriate time, and as just mentioned, credit is given to those with the best intuitive or spiritual awareness for the re-ception of the information. Do not confuse this with information only being given to the enlightened. Many of you have wonderful awareness without much enlightenment. (good intuition without spiritual knowledge).

What I will tell you now has to do with Earth disease. I will not specify which disease, and I will be very general. The information, however, is timely and appropriate. That is to say that it is correct for some of you to know now, and it is being given by others like the Kryon at this time. <u>It will require work and discovery to implement, but the basics are here.</u>

Living disease organisms on Earth are made of very small strings of repeating parts. These parts come together with symmetry and form to produce a system that is designed to perpetuate itself, and specifically to match up to human systems when appropriate, and to bring about further imbalance and often death. I have already spoken of the universal appropriateness of this, and how the karmic imprint and implants respond to disease. Please understand that these things are not mistakes in the universal scheme, but rather are very important and correct mechanisms for your complex interaction of expression on the planet.

Within the symmetry of repeating parts that make up the whole disease organism there are specific parts that are special. These specific parts have extensions and depressions which "look" for the opposite extensions and depressions within similar systems in the human body. Like a deadly key in a lock, if the extensions and depressions fit each other from disease organism to human organism, then the disease attaches itself and begins to grow. As an enlightened human, if you are paying attention now, and you are able to truly understand what is being presented here, you will have an understanding of how your karmic imprint is applied at the cellular level. For the shape of the extensions and depressions in the many systems of your personal biology is like a lock, ready to see a "key" for the disease organism.... or not. A significant implant can change your lock, therefore, and void the ability of the key to open it – and healing and balance will occur. Think of your implant, therefore, as a lock-out against disease.

Most of you arrive with an imprint that is likely to allow disease. It is always your karmic implant that voids these things. This is simply part of overall human karma relating to the Earth when you come in. Many of you are also given various implants at birth to void the general imprint parameters (why some humans get disease and some don't).

It is not up to human science to ever have the ability to change the imprint. It simply will never be within your ability, for it is not a biological process. Therefore, logically there are only two methods that will help you. (1) For you personally: a change in your implant from the universe, as has been described in the writings to this point, and (2) For the planet: a method to alter the disease so the key is changed, and no longer is able to fit any human system.

Know this: Even after the key in is the lock, it is not too late to change things. This is because, (1) the key is constantly growing new keys that continue to mate to other locks within the body, and (2) the key is never in the lock for good. Disease is an unnatural unbalanced state. To remain this way, even mated keys and locks must continue to "interrogate" one another to see if they still match. If you understand the meaning of this, then you will understand how healing works, even when it is too late. I will be specific later in this writing as to some of the workings of the symmetry of repeating parts that make up the whole disease organism.

Healing in The New Energy

In the new energy you have the power to heal as never before. It is thus: When you are in balance and love, and you come in contact with an unbalanced human entity who is receptive to your power, then you may approach and do the "spiritual interrogation" (*healing*). This is where the one touches the other, and in an instant of time, the one spiritually interrogates the other on an astral level (the highest level possible). The question is asked from soul to soul, and the question is: **"Is it universally appropriate at this time for your imprint to be altered to change your locks? If so, you have the permission to use the Love source power to change your own karma and respond to this inquiry by <u>healing yourself.</u>"** Notice that the entity is given permission by the power of the balanced entity to heal itself. The power of the balanced entity is not used to actually heal, but as a catalyst or prompter to give the other the go ahead. This is significant, and I hope its meaning is not lost on you as the reader at this time.

You might say: Why would any unbalanced humans answer "no" to permission to use the power within to heal themselves? This is where the universal wisdom of appropriateness comes in, as described in the past writings, where we as powerful soul entities decide our own lessons collectively before we arrive at an expression on Earth. As a "piece of God" we use the love source to decide what the imprint should be like, so as to learn the lessons that in turn will raise the vibrations of Earth. In a later writing I will describe to you the difference between the much misunderstood *predestination* concept, and what is really occurring here. Although you cannot truly understand the working of all of this, you are very able to grasp the intent of the truth, and what **is not** happening here. This may be important to some of you who have trouble understanding just how much control you have individually of your own fate while you are here.

If a soul feels that the lesson isn't learned yet, then it will turn down the opportunity to use the power to void the disease. A "turn down" is no reflection on the balanced human. Your concept of healing must now change to fit the new concept of giving permission to heal. When permission is accepted or declined, then the healing work has been done (*until the next time*). You also might ask: Why would a diseased human entity need to have permission in this manner? Why not just do it? If the karma isn't needed anymore, simply use the power and heal. The answer is simple: Remember that the human entity with the disease is unbalanced. Any unbalance at all is going to affect the whole. That is to say that you cannot have only one of the three unbalanced. Physical disease will affect the mind and spirit in a fashion that often makes communication with the astral almost impossible. This is why so many humans contact disease and die without hope. Once the disease has taken hold, there is often no more real spiritual communication. Ironically for you on Earth, when a diseased human knows that death is imminent there is often a huge attempt at spiritual reconciliation and balance. But the one demands the other: A real healing communication requires a spiritual balance, which isn't the case in a dying person with a physical disease. This is why balanced healers are so important on the planet – to help those who can't possibly "get through" because of the disease. Do you think you can't make a difference? Even your presence in a room with a physically diseased person can help... Believe it! Never walk away from an opportunity like this. Even if you feel it is of no value, and you can see no result, there is work being done.

Be aware also that life lessons and karma are often at work here to prevent the healing, and that is the subject of this communication. For in many cases it is appropriate to terminate, or to carry the suffering on for a time; so the answer to the soul's healing inquiry would be "no." Do the work and move on. Don't feel that you failed if the person does not respond. But be aware that for as many who do not respond there will be as many who do... and this is where you get to change the energy for the planet.

Therefore a healer in the new energy "intervenes" with what has been the past process, and gives permission to the unbalanced one to use the balance needed from the love source to create internal balance again. If it is correct, and the timing is appropriate, then the unbalanced ones can heal themselves. The good news here is that in the coming years you will be able to heal many (give them permission to balance themselves) who would otherwise have to terminate and return. **This is part of the transmutation of energy** process that I spoke of. For the difference you will create by allowing this shortcut for other humans will in itself speed up the timing of the whole, therefore transmuting the negative energy that always accompanies human death in the form of sorrow, emotional trauma and intense karmic interaction – not to mention the process of taking the time to grow up again and fulfill the next expression's goals. Can you see how this is so? This in effect is erasing negative energy that would have been in the future but never comes to fruition, and allows the positive to continue to grow without being knocked back. In the astral the future is now, and therefore the healing will have positive planetary results now. If this is difficult for you to understand, think of stored up energy in a battery. It is stored for the future, for a future event; but it is positive, real energy now in the form of electricity within the battery. Therefore it exits within the now, even though it will also have future impact when it is finally used.

There are human souls with diseased bodies right now expecting you to arrive and intervene, and the answer from within the soul will be yes, YES... believe it! Can you think of a better way to use the love source than this?

Changing The Disease Organism

I spoke of the workings of the symmetry of repeating parts that make up the whole disease organism. As I admonished earlier, the

Kryon cannot give answers that you must work for, and sometimes answers are purposefully given that must be understood through further meditation, in that they are metaphoric. It is not my intention to ever be evasive or put you through any stress, or cause you to launch action based on misinformation, for I love you dearly and respect your soul as I respect the love source itself!

Within the symmetry of the very small repeating parts that make up the whole disease organism there are only a few parts that make up the "key" as described before. These parts have very special properties. Not only are they the only ones with extensions and depressions that "look" for matching patterns at the cellular level, but **they are sensitive to magnetic interference**. Within the string of repeating parts, magnetics are very specific. Certainly this cannot surprise you if you have followed the writings of the Kryon. My very presence here is to alter the magnetic attributes that you have lived in all your lives so that you can enjoy more power. This is fine tuning your spirituality at the very cellular level that I am speaking of.

You must (1) expose the string of parts, (2) identify the parts in question, and (3) change them magnetically, to be successful. Be aware that an overall barrage of magnetic energy in a random fashion will not work. For all properties will change in the identical proportion, retaining balance to each other even though the overall polarity might be altered. The key will remain unchanged. You must change the balance between the parts themselves within the string. This will have the result similar to taking a key and removing one of the depressions... then it will no longer fit the lock.

When you have accomplished this task, then continue to apply this same method to other Earth environmental problems... specifically the problem of your nuclear waste. Unstable elements can be totally neutralized. It is not necessary to have this volatile matter exist with you on the planet. Although this is not biological, it still exhibits unbalance in nature, and much of it is not naturally occurring. Using the same methods of specific magnetic particle intervention and repolarization, you will be able to succeed. Your future technology will allow for this, for when you are able to discover the mechanics, you will be able to process the particle alteration on a large scale. You have earned this! Also be aware that your planet's biology can be used to help.

I am Kryon of magnetic service.
You all are dearly loved!

Kryon

There is no greater new power than that of
verbalization and visualization.

These two combined will create purpose and
substance where nothing existed before
but negativity and darkness.

With this in mind, how can you
be still?

Chapter Six

Jesus Christ

Jesus Christ
Chapter Six

The Metaphysical Christ

This is a brief treatise on the Metaphysical view of Jesus Christ, and also a quick look at what Metaphysicians believe. It has been channelled, (offered within the responsibility of divine spirit) in the purest sense of love by the entity Kryon. This was the first channel, and is written from the perspective of the writer passing on the Kryon consciousness, as apposed to a direct channel as in the first person of the Kryon (as you have been reading thus far).

It is not meant to convince, defend, or otherwise foster any cause or belief system. If you disagree with these thoughts, or are uncomfortable reading these views, then you should stop reading and return to what you feel is correct for you. If you continue, the information may serve you.

In the western world (known as the "first world"), which takes in all of the Americas and most of Europe, Jesus Christ is probably one of the best known names of all. To many the name Jesus represents tremendous personal joy, and it would be difficult to speak of Him or discuss Him without bringing up very strong feelings and emotions. This is as it should be.

From the time most of us in the first world were old enough to understand anything, we were told about Jesus. It didn't matter if you were a Christian or not; you knew about Jesus. The poem "One Solitary Life" indicates that no other person who ever walked the Earth had anywhere near the impact that Jesus did.

Christmas in the first world is a very special time of year, anticipated by all. If you are a Jew, or any other non-Christian, you have to go out of your way to get around it, and almost everyone is bombarded by it. This makes Jesus' birthday the most special, well-publicized event of the year. The Jews are taught that the Messiah has not yet come, but will come in the future, and the Christians are assured that He has not only been here, but died for the sins of the world... and will be returning to set up a special world order.

Unfortunately through the last 2,000 years, hundreds of Christian sects developed, all with their own ideas of what Jesus said and meant, and how a human should live the good life of a true believer. It was common that each sect thought its own doctrine was more correct than the others, and that each had its own spiritual verification to prove its own claims.

Some of the variations put emphasis on worshiping Jesus' Mother as much as Him. Some put emphasis on what they felt were secrets that only believers could know, told only in secret ceremony to a selected few. Some felt that you had to "sign up" and make a commitment, and join a group to be a believer, and some felt that it was good enough to just accept Jesus in your heart. Some felt that the prophets from two thousand years ago were the only prophets that were valid, and some felt that the church still had on-going prophets. One or two felt that there should be a supreme Christian leader, but the rest felt that local leaders were good enough. Some felt that only very special men could communicate with Jesus, and that the common man had to go through the special ones, confessing wrong-doings to the special ones who could talk to God – and the special ones could never be women. Some felt that anyone could talk to Jesus directly. Some felt that only a handful of men would be chosen to be with Him in the end... naturally from their sect. Some felt that slightly less than 200,000 souls would be chosen to be with Him in the end... again from their own followers. Others felt that anyone who believed the "correct way" could make it; then they carefully dictated the "correct way." Some said that you couldn't be married to be a spiritual leader; some said it didn't matter. Some said you couldn't live in western society or have any money and be a leader; some said it didn't matter. Others insisted that you had to believe that Jesus' birth was a miracle in order to worship Him (He wouldn't listen otherwise); others said it didn't matter, that anyone could worship Him (and He would listen to anyone).

Many of the original scripture meanings were verified from the Dead Sea Scrolls discovered recently. These very important writings have been sequestered for 50 years, however, and only certain authorized scholars from a certain group have been appointed to study them. A very few men still control who can see them. (This will change soon, with some startling revelations.)

It was very common to disagree about Jesus, and what a human was supposed to do with His teachings. Almost without exception, however, everyone believed that Jesus was the representation of the essence of the **love** of God. He was love itself, and had come to Earth in a very special way, as a supernatural individual, to teach. No one who believed that Jesus had been here missed that part. However, the details of what to do with the knowledge, and which group to join, was so intensely debated that many so-called Holy wars were fought in the name of Jesus, and many innocent humans were killed because they were allied with identified unbelievers. Even today you have to be very careful in certain English speaking countries in Europe when confronted by guards asking which of two Christian sects you might belong to. The wrong answer could bring you harm.

Explaining all this to a visitor just arriving from another planet might be somewhat unsettling. (Actually, explaining anything to a space visitor might be unsettling!) Not to suggest that we will be explaining this to a space visitor, but just as an example... And if that visitor happened to be knowledgeable on Earth history and culture and current events, it might be hard to justify the importance of Jesus. The visitor might bring up the fact that the **majority of the human population** of the Earth worships one or two other "supernatural" individuals, and although there are many sects represented here as well, there is a much better unification of how to worship God. Millions of humans all unite to pray at the same time, give thanks to God and go about their lives without the knowledge of Jesus at all. And the truly embarrassing part for Jesus' followers is that these others take their belief system with them in a way that is highly impressive. Spend some time with a middle Eastern Third World person for a while and compare how much time they give their worship, or the sacrifices they endure. Spend time with an Asian person and observe the same thing; then with a modern first world Christian believer. The comparison will leave you with some highly poignant questions about faith.

Of course if you ask Christian leaders about this, they will say all the others (most of the Earth's population) are wrong. They are heathens, and because they do not know of Jesus, they are lost souls. It is up to Christians to bring them the good news (about Jesus). The Christians are taught that God selected Jesus to come to Earth and speak to only a very select group of European Caucasians, living in a section of what we now call the Middle East. And this group (or those in it that believed Him) had the task to carry His teachings to the 4 billion others around the globe in the span of time before He returned.

The truly ironic thing about all this is that the others that do not "know" Jesus, worship their own supernatural individuals based on some of the very same premises that Christians use in their own worship of Jesus. In fact (unbelievably) some of the "scriptures" of these heathen believers are very similar in teaching to that of the Holy Bible! Most of the Sermon on the Mount and classic Old Testament commandments are clearly covered in principal and intent in all the other world writings. Some of them read as though they were lifted right out of the Christian scriptures, but some were written considerably before Jesus arrived... and some during the missing years of Jesus life. Strangest of all is the fact that the others believe that their teachers were also the representation of the essence of the love of God, and that they had also come to Earth in miraculous ways as supernatural individuals to teach and do miracles while on the Earth (just like the Christians feel about Jesus). By the way, if you ask these others, Christians are the heathens! and "unbelievers." (Be very careful not to write a book that might disagree with them; they may hunt you down and kill you.)

It is the Metaphysical belief that Jesus Christ was one of the highest ascended masters ever to visit the Earth. He came to give us truth, love and example. While He was here many wrote down what He did, giving us a terrific record of His stay here. After He left many "channelled" His teachings from "spirit" (they called it the Holy Spirit), giving instruction in truth and love. Some of these channellings are the books of the New Testament, translated and re-translated many times and passed down through men for 2,000 years. Metaphysicians also believe that other masters, perhaps as powerful – perhaps even Jesus Himself – appeared as other masters, visiting the other cultural parts of the Earth that needed to see the exterior of someone like themselves. He/they brought basically the same universal love message with each visit. (Some also feel that Jesus did not die, and continued teaching after He left the Middle East.)

Christians will tell you that since scripture (channelling) is often confusing, you have to trust the Holy Spirit ("Spirit") to give you wisdom to understand. To the Metaphysician, this is simply saying that the same Spirit that gave the writings will give the meanings. Again, most religious leaders in power cannot begin to agree with what Spirit says, or who is even qualified to listen! This leads to the enormous fragmentation of the organized followers of Jesus.

To the Metaphysician, the most unfortunate part of the whole historic event of Jesus' visit is what **men** in power made of it. Jesus' words were translated and interpreted to seemingly demean and tear down the spirit and the will of man; i.e., "no man is worthy"... "we are born into sin"... "everyone falls short"... "there is nothing you personally can do to lift yourself out of your unworthiness"... "the spirit of man is sin"... "you are born with the legacy of going to Hell when you die"... "since you can't do anything worthy, you have to give over your responsibility to a higher power"... "if things go great for you, then you had nothing to do with it." Christians are taught very early that you have to turn your life (power) over to Jesus to lift you out of this mire that is your own human unworthiness. Men were supposed to have killed the Son of God. They teach that guilt is <u>expected</u> and sorrow is <u>appreciated</u> by God. Forgiveness by God follows, and the metaphor of Jesus being the Shepherd and the humans being the sheep is repeated over and over in the scriptures. (Sheep, as you know, are not expected to do any thinking for themselves.)

This concept is the biggest void of belief between the Metaphysical Jesus and the Christian's Jesus. Metaphysicians don't believe that Jesus meant this at all. They don't believe that Jesus wanted to be worshiped as a Deity either. His words mean something entirely different to those who embrace this new universal belief, and His reported death does not have the same significance.

Metaphysical people believe that each person is born into the world as a spiritual-based human being with the total power of God within, just waiting to be used through spiritual understanding. They also feel that each person is responsible for his own life and his own power. Turning your life over to God is not to lose control, but to <u>take</u> control, using the teachings of Jesus (and others) as a guide, to give you the power that was yours all along. Jesus didn't come to make us sheep. He came to give instructions on how to awaken the shepherd in each of us! This is called "taking your power."

Metaphysicians are concerned with the **here and now** (even though there is often a great deal of spectacular publicity on the ancillary sidelines such as past lives, UFOs and psychic phenomena). The real Metaphysician is concerned with self-improvement through the study of how to use the universal laws taught by Jesus (and others) to lift themselves to a higher consciousness while on Earth... another way of saying that they believe they can have better lives, and have peace, health and joy while on Earth, through tapping into the power of God which is available for **all** (as taught by Jesus). At the same time they do this, they are helping to raise the consciousness of the planet through prayer, the real object of our time on Earth.

This universal kind of belief could simply be viewed as just another sect, another one of the hundreds of diverse ones that exist now. So what's the difference? Are Metaphysical people just another group who feel they know God better than the rest? Then they are no different than the others! Perhaps this could be true, but on inspection, note the unique differences of Metaphysical belief: • All other human beliefs are respected. – • No other system is made "wrong." – • Metaphysicians are not evangelical. – • They are not "Doctrine driven;" the specifics are often left up to the individual. – • There is no human power center. – • Rules are self-imposed and governed only by the individual, and • For the most part they believe in and practice the universal love teachings of Jesus.

The Metaphysical Belief System Briefly Summarized

The actual word Metaphysics is fairly intangible. A popular Thesaurus gives these examples of words that refer to Metaphysics:

metaphysical:	Thesaurus
adj.	**spiritual**, bodiless, celestial, disembodied, ethereal, heavenly, incorporeal, insubstantial, intangible, nonmaterial, unearthly, unreal, unsubstantial;
∞	**weird**, bizarre, eerie, ghostly, incredible, mystical, odd, ominous, spooky, strange, supernatural, uncanny, unearthly.

Since the words *bizarre, odd, spooky, strange* and *supernatural* made it to the official Thesaurus... you can imagine the impression most people have of the Metaphysician! Here is a brief description of what Metaphysical people are really about.

(1) To a Metaphysician God is a concept that refers to a unified collective consciousness of all of us together (the great "I AM"). This means that each human is a piece of God. While on Earth, however, this fact is veiled from the individual. This very veil is described in the Holy Bible in First Corinthians 13:12 (the great love chapter which beautifully describes love in the universal scheme of things). In this verse it is noted that we see the truth as though through a darkened glass, and that only when we are face to face (one with God) will we know everything. The beauty of the translation in the King James version is that it is very Metaphysical: *"..but then shall I know even as also I am known"* This is to say that the *knower* is also the *known,* an unmistakable tie to the God entity within each of us. Many think that to believe we each have the power of God is ridiculous; but the prophet John clearly stated that each one of us has the **power to become as Jesus**: a "son" of God, one who is born or begotten of the main Spirit (John 1:12).

So what's the point? If we are God, who's running the show while we are here? The answer, and perhaps a confusing one: **we are**. As part of God we decided to come here, and we collectively agreed on the lessons to be presented. When we leave, we will collectively judge ourselves and our performance, and continue towards a goal of perfect, complete love energy for the entire universe. This is why Metaphysical people are always saying there are no accidents. Things happen for reasons. Children die... wars take place... people are healed... all within the scope of what is supposed to happen for the benefit of those humans who are here to learn. It's a big school with many levels. Our time here is but a blink of an eye to the whole scheme. While we are here, we get help from others who have agreed to come with us, that perhaps are unseen, (Spooky, huh? More on this later.)

It might not make sense to a logical human mind that we actually decided to come to Earth to go through a life of potential suffering and hardship, but to the mind of God (us when we are not here), it is as it should be, and we came in love to go through something that will help **all of us**. Make no mistake, however, that while we are here, Metaphysicians also believe we can manifest anything we choose through the power we inherently have as a part of God when we get here (John 1:12 again). It's back to the lessons, and all people on Earth can "plug in" to the power any time they are ready.

All this leads to questions of possible past lives, karmic group involvements, predestination and all the other extra topics that have been associated with the Metaphysician (perhaps out of proportion to the real intent of the belief). These extra things are not doctrine. They are important to the individual to the degree the individual feels that they apply, and how they directly relate to what the individuals should do with the information in order to help himself. Most Metaphysical people, however, end up believing that they indeed were on Earth, or somewhere else in the universe many times, and that this Earthly life, like each of the others (which continue to be veiled while they occur), are lessons, or tests with a purpose of the eventual elevation of all humanity to a level of enlightenment that will be very God-like in itself, similar to the description found in Revelation 21 in the Holy Bible of the "new heaven and Earth," where at the end of earthly time, we will have the final "marriage of the lamb." (The lamb refers to Jesus as the sacrifice in love that God made in sending Him to Earth to suffer at the hands of men.) This marriage to the Metaphysician is the graduation from the lessons, the final chapter, and the time where those with enlightened minds actually will have the veil removed while <u>on Earth</u>. And yes, they will meet Jesus again, and all will recognize each other. Others not ready will be removed; this is the source of the dark parts of Revelation. There will be a battle to be fought, but not of the sort you might expect. Many will die, however, again in the plan that we have all agreed on in advance. Metaphysicians believe that at the "cellular level" (a way of saying "in our hearts") we know everything that has ever happened to us since the beginning of time as we understand it.

(2) The Metaphysical system embraces all of humanity, and sees it as one homogeneous group in **real time** (instead of seeing humanity in terms of groups of humans for harvest, or lost individuals to pray for or to send missionaries to, etc.). A real time arena provides for interaction right now; that is, what happens in China today affects the spiritual aspects of all humanity today, including the hot-dog vendor in New York or the Pope. If the time is right, and enough people pray together, unbelievable events can take place – such as the almost overnight removal of the wall in Berlin, or dramatic changes in Russia, or peace in South America or the Middle East. These events are <u>universal driven</u> events, not based in one religion, but they are responsive to the working of universal mechanics such as prayer (meditation) and love, present and practiced among many religions. They are also proof that we are closing in on our goal for a unified Earth.

(3) Metaphysics makes no person or group of persons "wrong." It is a way of relating to God and the universe, not a set of rules for salvation. It is very personal. Membership in a group is not necessary. In the competitive first world this is a difficult concept to understand; an example would be if you were in a school of many different grade levels, all studying in a parallel fashion for the same diploma. Certain individuals might want unique elective courses or difficulty levels to accomplish the same education. Some of the other grades might be competitive or closed, but all going toward the same goal. Students would select the grade level and course that fits their needs for the moment, or that puts them with others of their culture or like mind. Graduation would be terrific! with everyone gathering for a common celebration at the very end, all celebrating in love and harmony at the task accomplished. The Metaphysical grade level's "signature" is that they would help cheer the others toward their goal, instead of insisting that their Metaphysical grade was best, or that theirs was the only correct path. In other words it is one of the only systems that acknowledges that **all** the other systems have a right to exist, and are correct in context with what many people must go through for their time on Earth.

(4) Metaphysicians believe that the mechanics of meditation, prayer and love are universal, and work **no matter who you are**. That's why **most** of the other spiritual belief systems of the world regularly "hook in" to so many of the benefits of their works, such as instant, positive results from prayer, as well as remarkable healing and success. Many miracles are seen daily in the third world (unreported and unknown to the first world) through a regular practice of prayer and meditation. Holy Men are alive today that are helping people to see the power in themselves, their meetings regularly resulting in dozens of healings.

(5) Because of number 3 and 4 (above), Metaphysics is not evangelical. It is one of the only systems on Earth that is not. If you

are ready for it, then you will embrace it. If you are not, then you will not. Naturally there is the idea that those who embrace it are more enlightened than those who do not, but this is a human judgment, *and tells you a great deal about humans, not God.* Metaphysicians believe in spreading the news, but not converting anyone with it.

(6) Finally, and most painful to most Christians, is the obvious fact that Metaphysicians do not consider Jesus to be God any more than you or I. They do not worship Him as God, and they do not believe that Jesus wanted them to. They **do believe** that Jesus was perhaps closer to God, or pure love, than any other entity in existence in the universe, and that His visit to Earth was monumental and critical for humanity. He was of the very highest enlightened level that ever was, and He came to teach us during a time when it was absolutely necessary for that part of civilization... and He came with full knowledge that He would suffer painfully at the end of His tenure. It was a collective decision to send Him, and a painful one. Did He do all of the reported miracles? Yes. Did He come back from the dead? He certainly had the power. Was He the **Son** of God? Inasmuch as we can understand what that means, yes. (We cannot know the mind of God any more than we can explain the workings of the internal combustion engine to an anteater! There are things that are simply beyond our ability to know while we are here.) When God wished to make known the emotional feelings of just how important and special Jesus was to the whole, the reference to the relationship of a human-born child was used as the closest thing that humans could relate to. There simply is nothing more special to humans than their offspring. Jesus exemplified the absolute power and love of God available to everyone. It is also possible that He might have visited other worlds as well. Just think of this possibility; this speculation alone should heighten a person's love and admiration for this very special being we call Jesus.

Why was He a **man**? Since He had to be one sex or the other to come as a human, it was more acceptable for the culture of that time for Jesus to appear as a male. God knew it would be easier for Him to teach and be listened to by the elders. ...As to the obvious masculine references of God, and Son of God and Son of Man, these were also "genderized" by the writers of the time (probably without much thought) to conform to the conception of acceptable power and authority. Is God **male**? NO. Do the clouds have sex organs? Is the air we breathe male? God is spirit, generic and universal. Our reference to female and male is relative only to our time on Earth. For these reasons many Metaphysicians refer to God as "Mother-Father God" or just "Spirit." Now is an age where women and men are finally coming together and recognizing, perhaps for the first time, that they share a common spirituality that has no specific gender domination. This is also the time for the emergence of a known, but not necessarily *first world* concept, of bonding for couples on the highest level possible: that of the spiritual first (God Love), then of human love, then the physical.

Metaphysicians also believe that a great deal of the bible was interpreted and translated by men for men's purposes, and that there were even parts left out on purpose (this will be proven on Earth eventually, but not necessarily accepted by Christians). Metaphysicians don't believe in the devil in the classic sense. Hell and eternal damnation do not play a traditional part in the belief either (see "the unseen" on page 140). They point out that before Christianity became known as we know it today, it passed through a time when powerful governments controlled it, manipulated it and used it even for war. The power seats were most often the religious leaders, and they were often corrupt. Scriptures were omitted, edited and translated in ways that helped control people, and those very areas are still read and followed today. You can't get into a "bible thumping" contest with a Metaphysician. They simply do not believe the bible is totally accurate, and therefore what is sacred and authoritative to one person cannot be used to qualify or prove a point to the other. It becomes a spitting contest, and no one wins. Metaphysicians use the bible as a reference to many general truths as spoken by Jesus, and they believe that in its original condition it was "channelled" (given by God through humans)... all of it, not just the parts you have seen.

Metaphysicians rely on **meditation.** Meditation is simply prayer – while listening instead of speaking – and nothing more. It isn't spooky or strange, and it isn't necessary to be in the lotus position or hum strange noises while you do it. Meditation is where you receive power, intuitive information and direction. Metaphysicians also believe very strongly in prayer (speaking, worship and dialogue), used basically for helping others. They believe Spirit (The Holy Spirit) is the voice of the collective God, and that it is just as powerful today as ever, and it will provide good information as it is supposed to be provided. It is on-going and did not stop with the prophets 2,000 years ago. The Trinity (Father, Son, Holy Ghost) is replaced with the concept of equal power for all, not just a three-way-split.

God is love, and love is the most powerful force in the universe. More and more, love will replace law and grace as God's method of working on Earth as we approach the end of the term. The higher levels of enlightenment will allow for it. When we are finished the pure love energy will prevail, and Jesus, as well as the other great masters of all recorded history, will walk with humans on the Earth again. This will be spectacular, since it will signal the lifting of the veil on the Earth while the humans are still here! Metaphysicians feel that our world is simply one of many to have this happen, and that each time it happens, it is a very special event, helped and celebrated all over the universe by all kinds of spiritual entities (many of whom we are ignorant of, but that have been helping us all along). No human really has any concept of the real power of the love energy.

The "Unseen"

So much has been made of the "unseen" aspect of Metaphysics that it takes on a pseudo importance to many. What about ghosts, angels, UFOs, spirit guides, etc.? It is **not necessary** for any of us to know about anything more than *why we are here*, and *what we are supposed to do* (that should keep us busy all our lives!). The mechanics of the universe, and of the way things work, is given to us peripherally and in small doses. Suffice it to say that it **is not** that important to understand it all. If the car gets you there, it isn't necessary to understand all about the engine to arrive safely. Some of us desire to be mechanics, however, and those are honored with explanations and further teachings.

For those of you who desire to know more, there are volumes of writings on this subject. But **here are some basic truths**: There are many, many spiritual entities (like us) that are in many other Earth scenarios. Some are separate and independent of our purposes on Earth, and some directly support what we are supposed to be doing here. Yes, there are others on other worlds; (does that really shock you?) Some are like us, and are going through other lessons (lower and higher than our own). Others are not like us at all, and are not nearly as tangible as what we are used to, and therefore are startling to perceive. Some can marginally communicate. Some try, and shouldn't. Some visit, and some shouldn't.

Occasionally we cross paths with some of the other entities, sometimes as part of a master plan and sometimes unrelated to our lessons. Most often we become temporarily aware of being watched, or we feel communication has been given. Those are the episodes that relate to our time here, and are special – **and normal**. Other times we might see or hear things that may be frightening and not understood (like ghosts for instance). This is not that uncommon, and there are many who understand the mechanics of this. It is normal, but again, it isn't necessary for us to understand it. Even the bible speaks of spirits. It would not be logical to discount them.

Metaphysicians do not believe in the devil, or Hell. They believe these ideas and concepts were enhanced out of metaphorical biblical references to control people in a political way through the years. Make no mistake, however: there is definitely a spiritual dark side. Jesus came to teach us about that as well, and the admonition was clear: **Stay away from it!** You can just as easily manifest negativity and tragedy as love and healing. Your power as a piece of God is absolute... think about it. During the age of "law" on the Earth, God **created** a great deal of death and suffering. Not all that is manifested is beautiful and loving.

Casting out evil spirits is real. There are low unseen entities that will move into a negative space when invited. Deep depression and personality shutdown is a classic invitation syndrome. Sometimes it takes several of us together to accomplish a removal of those entities from another person, since the other person becomes almost powerless to help. Much of the time, however, mental illness and biological chemical imbalances are labeled as "possession by evil entities." It seems to be more spectacular to say that the Devil made them do it. Hearing voices is most likely to be a biological imbalance instead of a spiritual imbalance. Abnormal brain function can easily generate basal thought signals that are allowed to reverse themselves and travel back to the hearing center so that a person actually "hears" voices generated by this involuntary thought (This is similar to diodes failing in an electrical circuit, which keep current flowing in one direction.) Although frightening and often tragic, it isn't the work of the devil, or other spirits.

Our purpose on Earth is to transmute the negative to the positive, both in our own lives through the teachings of Jesus, and for the entire planet. <u>Love is king,</u> and is far more powerful; but the absence of love is sin. The incredible blackness of that state is hate, jealously, self-service, greed, power mongering and uncaring. Jesus came to Earth to give us the teachings that would allow us to lift ourselves out of that condition by way of the facts about who we really are, and how we can take our power and heal the planet. We are also told to spread the word, to give out the truth so that everyone can hear it. (Metaphysicians do not believe we were also instructed to force everyone to accept it.) The truth **will** make you free. Not everyone is ready for it, however, and should not be force fed. This is why a Metaphysician may inform you of what the system is about, then leave you alone. Some will walk away thinking the Metaphysicians are crazy, and others will become enlightened.

Words about Jesus' Teaching

The words about what Jesus taught are sacred; the <u>translations</u> are not (whatever you have been told). Translations are still forthcoming (like the ones that follow). Be open to understand these fresh interpretations; they are important. Below are some of the most powerful Holy Bible verses written by Jesus' followers, or attributed to Jesus Himself. They have been interpreted through "Spirit" (the Holy Spirit) by way of Kryon.

John 3:16 – written by John

"For God so loved the world, that He gave his only begotten Son, that whosoever believeth in Him should not perish, but have everlasting life."

The Metaphysician's view (John 3:16)

"For God so loved the people of Earth, it was decided to send the only qualified spiritual entity of the universe, Gods' highest being, actually born of the Spirit to walk among humans so that whoever listened to him and believed in the things He said, would not continue to be mired in Earth's negative ways, subject to die without enlightenment, but rather have the knowledge that would bring about life that will be without end."

John 1:11 & 12 – written by John

"He came unto his own, and his own received him not. But as many as received him, to them gave the power to become the sons of God, even to them that believe on his name:"

The Metaphysician's view

"He came to Earth and was with men who were just like him, and they did not recognize him and did not believe him. But as many as did believe his words and put them into practice, they received the unlimited knowledge and power to become exactly as He was – born as a child of God."

John 1:14 – written by John

"... And the Word was made flesh, and dwelt among us (and we beheld his glory, the glory as of the only begotten of the Father), full of grace and truth."

The Metaphysician's view

"And the truth of the universe was sent in the form of a human man to dwell among those of Earth. (and we saw him, and knew He spoke the truth, and we saw the glory of his love of the universe as represented by its highest form possible: the only one chosen from God) full of love and truth."

Romans 3:23 – written by Paul

"For all have sinned, and come short of the glory of God; being justified freely by his grace through the redemption that is in Christ Jesus:"

The Metaphysician's view

"All humans, in their negativity and ignorance, have fallen short of the knowledge, enlightenment and love that could have been theirs; this can now be changed, being freely offered by God through the love and truth brought to Earth by Jesus; the chosen one."

Romans 6:23 – written by Paul

"For the wages of sin is death; but the gift of God is eternal life through Jesus Christ our Lord."

The Metaphysician's view

"The result of staying in negativity and darkness without love is to die without enlightenment; but the free gift from God of Jesus will bring about light, power and eternal life through his love and teachings."

Romans 10:9 – written by Paul

"That if thou shalt confess with thy mouth the Lord Jesus and shalt believe in thine heart that God hath raised him from the dead, thou shalt be saved."

The Metaphysician's view

"When you openly acknowledge and verbalize the universal teachings and love of Jesus, and believe He had the power to raise Himself from the dead, you will have the enlightenment, understanding and power that will allow you to do the same."

John 14:5-7 – written by John, quoting Jesus

"Thomas saith unto him, Lord, we know not wither thou goest; and how can we know the way? Jesus saith unto him, I am the way, the truth, and the life: no man cometh unto the Father, but by me. If ye had known me, ye should have known my Father also: and from henceforth ye know him, and have seen him."

The Metaphysician's view

"Thomas said to Jesus: Lord, we don't know where you are going, so how can we possibly know how to proceed ourselves? Jesus told Thomas: I have shown you the way by giving you the truth and by the example of my life. No one can possibly come to God unless it is through my teachings and my spirit, for I am one with God. If you had recognized me, you would have recognized God within me; so from now on, you can say that you saw God, and you know Him."

Chapter Summary:

The Metaphysical beliefs are often referred as the **new age** movement. The associated paraphernalia often include crystals, energy modules, subliminal teachings, UFOs, Astrology and other seemingly unproven intangibles. A great many humans are attracted to anything unusual, and many are very hungry for answers other than those offered by the traditional church. In a movement where there is no central control, there is much of this "automatic" following, like moths to a flame. It unfortunately attracts the kooks, as well as those wishing for greater enlightenment.

All those who decide to further explore this system must understand the fact that they will have to wade through the weirdness, and that they must have the **power to discern** truth from fantasy, to separate the real believers from the commercial exploiters, or those who are there because they are confused, or because they are unbalanced. (There is also a great attraction of the unbalanced to the Christian belief; just ask any Christian minister.) Let the teachings of Jesus be the guide: View each person and look for the love and intelligent, mature spirit that <u>must</u> be there.

The "weird" eventually becomes "less weird" as people grow in the system, and gradually understand Metaphysics. Unexplained things are not necessarily all fake or weird: A pocket calculator brought to a meeting in Virginia 200 years ago would be unexplained and weird (and you might be burned at the stake for having it!). This item obviously is not either evil or fake, just not yet understood, and ahead of its time. Much of the Metaphysician's weirdness falls into this very category of "not yet understood, but working".

In the early days of human civilization we named our relationship with the universe (God) the dispensation of "law." Just like a stern parent, God set down the rules and punished those who misbehaved. When the man touched the Ark of the Covenant, he died, just like God said he would if he touched the power center... cause and effect, crime and punishment. This came as a result of how the universe dealt with the conscious level of that time, with Earth being in its infancy as a developing spiritual group. Those who had an especially elevated spiritual sense were removed: Elijah for instance, who was reported as "taken" without dying. Speaking to God face to face seemed to be common, but the fear of God was great.

Two thousand years ago we got the age of Grace. This referred to the grace of God to have sent Jesus to give us the truth about how things really worked. It seems that the world was ready for knowledge of the actual use of the spiritual power for themselves. It was a move upward for humans, and a higher spiritual level was presented. This was actually the age of responsibility, since to have the knowledge is to be responsible to use it. In those days, this new belief was their "new age," and Jesus' teachings were met with the typical scorn and disbelief by the negative people in power (as is any move upward in Spiritual awareness).

We are now beginning to enter the age of Love. Again it is being called the *new age*. This will be the final arena, and all the turmoil we will have will be the clashes between those who feel it and those who don't. This will be the natural way to weed out the ones who are not supposed to stay for the graduation. This final dispensation demands that we have learned what Jesus taught, and gives tremendous power to those who understand and are responsible in the use of the pure love energy.

Born-again Christians are very well suited to the new age, since their entire belief is grounded in love. But depending on their doctrine, they may be very uncomfortable with the unfolding events, and may feel that the anti-Christ is represented in the form of many of the new-age leaders. This will be caused from a rather poor and controlling interpretation of Revelation as presented by the church for hundreds of years. They would do well to relax and let God lead the way, and not make decisions based on doctrine alone. This will be the time to take responsibility for individual faith, and have the discernment about what is actually happening around them, not what they were told might happen. If humans were to know exactly about the end times, God would not have chosen to make the writings of the end times so vague and mysterious. It is up to the individual to take responsibility for the discernment of spirit, not someone else's interpretation. **Do not believe** anyone who tells you that they have the authoritative interpretation of the end times' writings; it has not yet been given. We were admonished not to add writings to the original book of Revelation so that the writings would remain vague!

The love energy will become more and more intense. This will make some very comfortable, while some will not be able to make the adjustment. The earth will physically react to the new dispensation, and the earth's polarity will alter itself to accommodate to the new consciousness. (The polarity alteration has been equated to the opening of the sixth seal in the book of Revelation... but this is human speculation... or is it?)

> Whoever you are reading this, know this as truth:... Fear does not have to be a part in what is to come, and what is coming should not be feared. Love is the new great power, and love will protect and serve us in the new times. Jesus was the bringer of love energy to the world.. it is no wonder that we continue to love Him so much.

God Bless You!

Kryon

Chapter Seven

Writer's Summary

Writer's Summary
Chapter Seven

I cannot let the Kryon writings for book one come to a close without sharing some very biological (human) thoughts and observations. First, if you have gotten this far (and really read everything up to here), you are to be congratulated for your perseverance! As mentioned earlier, the writings are not always in the best English language form, and sometimes they are downright cryptic unless you are really involved in the work.

I as the channeller, however, found myself understanding all of it, and explaining it in greater detail to those around me who were interested and had questions. This also led to a few private counseling sessions, and then to group sessions. What I gleaned from the information at these sessions, plus my own personal experience in applying the Kryon information, is what follows here. If you want to apply the Kryon writings to your life, then read this last chapter. I think you will find it to be important, for it is my advice to humans from the human standpoint instead of the Kryon standpoint.

Calling For the Neutral Implant (spiritual release)

Do you wish to call for the guide change and neutral implant/ release? I have now seen this first hand in its best case... and its worse case, the best case being when someone who, for whatever reason, was able to obtain a guide change almost overnight! When interviewing this kind of person, it seemed that either (1) the change had been slowly coming to a head over a long period of time, and there had been a sluggish difficult struggle to a state where the individual was really ready for the information, and also for the implant, or (2) there was very strong trauma about the time of the request (such as a death, or a life threatening experience). This seemed to somehow accelerate the event. All this shows me that the guide change experience was outlined by Kryon in its worst case scenario so that we would not be surprised if that's what we got. It also showed me that the timing of the event is not quite as immediate as it may sound. That is, it might be, but it could also be something that has been in the works for a long time, much before you read the Kryon papers.

In the worst case I have indeed been with a person who exhibited all the classic symptoms as described in the writings. He was ready to leave Earth, and had nothing whatsoever to live for... not a state of depression over lost fortune or lost love, but a real feeling of completion without promise of anything to follow. He was done with his family, friends, profession and hobbies. Nothing interested him any longer. This was a real "neutralized person." Then something unexpected and unwritten (by Kryon) happened: this person suddenly became super sensitive to the state of the Earth. That is, all the injustice of man to man and man to Earth became overwhelmingly clear: and this added to his misery. It was almost like he was able to see the human race as God would see it, but without any of the love and tolerance to temper what was being experienced. This deepened the dark hole he was in. The only thing I could do was love him. His transition had to be his own. As I walked away from that experience I was sobered by the extent of what I had seen. I realized that I had gotten a peek into what I had only just written about through Kryon, and again I was struck by how timely it was. Fortunately this person also moved through this time, to emerge stronger and peaceful.

I have also been with a person who has just received the new guides, and she was literally bouncing off the walls with new energy and love enlightenment. Her experience leads me to give you advice about communicating with your guides. (Read on.)

Communicating with the Universe

If I could tell you one main thing about how the other side works with us, I would say they work *literally*. Many enlightened believers still think that the universe is like some kind of spiritual Santa Claus, who knows when your asleep or awake, or when you are bad or good... and that all you have to do is stand around and things will fall out of the sky for you. Well, there is actually some truth to this. If you are following your path, your windows of opportunity will indeed come along for you to walk through. There is much more, however, to consider here:

Know this: if the universe brings you through the guide change, and you are successfully transmuting negative to positive, the universe sees you as doing your job and fulfilling your contract. If you also happen to be starving at the same time, the universe isn't aware of it! How can this be (you might say)? Remember that you are biological, in lesson, in a small cultural goldfish bowl that is unique to humans. The universe **must be informed** what you need, and this is done by communicating to your guides. Odd as it may sound, all things non-spiritual must be asked for. The universe indeed knows what your next karmic lesson is, or what you must go through, or what neat opportunity is coming your way, but it must be informed about what you need to exist in the human goldfish bowl. First you need food! You get that though working for money (money is not a spiritual concept). Don't ask for specific scenarios; instead inform your guides about how it works in general where you are. Kryon was clear to remind us that the guides are our main link to the other side of the veil. Let them know that you need work, or the amount of money you require, or how the universe can help get you into a place where you are able to work less and earn more, etc. Don't be too specific about the "hows," or you'll limit the result, since it will be literal. Let them know what you need, but don't tell them how to do it for you. This is called co-creation.

The guides actually need to be talked to. Verbalize these things **out loud.** Listen to yourself say the words, (so that they sound correct); then stand back! You will absolutely get what you discussed. I have experienced this over and over. When I don't communicate, things become marginal. When I do, things start happening, and they happen in some of the least expected ways. Always continue the communication (almost like daily prayers), but don't forget to allow time for quiet listening as well.

My advice to those who receive new guides is to immediately start talking to them. First: if you don't, they will start working so fast within your head that you will feel like you are non-Earthly, and swear you are going to burn up. You have to let them know how fast they can do their work on your new implants... otherwise they will go at "warp speed," and you won't be able to function properly! The dear one I spoke to who had just received her new guides didn't know this. She was experiencing so much pressure in her head that she felt as though she was wearing a helmet! In addition the energy was coming so intently that occasionally she had to get up and leave the room when she was around other humans, because their energy clashed with the flow and gave her discomfort. None of these things are necessary if you simply inform your guides as to your needs. As a postscript to this admonition, I must tell you that being with a person who has just experienced this is a very rewarding experience. It can't help but uplift you... being with such fresh, new enlightenment. It gives me a glimpse into what it might be like to have gatherings of these people. Negativity won't have a chance.

Those of you who don't want anything to do with this new experience can still gain much by this basic universal new energy information. Kryon makes it clear that this new energy gives us new abilities. These new abilities are actually an intensification of self-awareness and realization. That is, we now have permission to do much more with that part of us that is the intrinsically powerful "piece of God" that Kryon speaks of, and the only way to use it is through the guides. We are blocked from using it ourselves (hence the offering of the neutral implant), but we can still become much more powerful... help people, and help ourselves through constant communication with our guides.

Good guide communication should be a book unto itself, since it does not seem to be intuitive, human behavior. The simple fast secret? Ask your guides for the best way! Start clumsily if necessary, and verbalize out loud that you need help finding the best way to communicate (see the next paragraph). Immediately start explaining what you need, both spiritually and physically. Remember, they are here to make things work for you. Their real purpose is to help you realize (bring to fruition) the communication so that you can move through your karmic interactions better. Use this newly improved conduit!

The most important part of guide communication is (guess what?) LOVE. You simply will not be able to communicate without it. Love your guides as you love God. Love them as you would love the best loved person, pet, or entity on Earth. Visualize yourself in their arms with everyone hugging everyone... then start your communication. You want results? This will bring it.

Imprints and Implants

Are you confused by these two names, and what they represent? If so, you are not alone. Many have asked me to explain this. Although Kryon gives good explanations throughout the book for both of these very important concepts, I feel that I can wrap up a more concise picture with the following words, and a chart to help.

Your **imprint** is the spiritual "fingerprint" you are born with. It is represented at the cellular level, and interacts with your DNA along with your biology. It cannot be changed. Examples of your imprint are: karmic lessons to be learned that you have scheduled for yourself, astrological birth influences (your magnetic balance birth sign), your star karma, your life lesson and your auric color. These are very important attributes, and reflect on your personality traits, ego, body type, emotional status, degree of immunity to disease and life line.

Although this **imprint** cannot be changed (ever), It can be **affected** or **neutralized** by an equally powerful spiritual instrument (see the next paragraph). Is this hard to understand? Picture this: The water pressure in your garden hose is always there. There is nothing you can do to change that. This pressure comes from a very large source and is always present. You can control it, or even void it completely, however, by installing a spigot. You therefore have added something in order to neutralize something.

Your **implant** is like the spigot. It tempers your imprint. Think of your implants as "restrictors," or *variable controls on your imprint.* Unlike the imprint they are constantly changing, and are the universe's clever way of allowing your guides access to your "spiritual engine." When you are born you have an entire set of implants that restrict certain aspects of your makeup. A typical human implant (as explained by Kryon) that we all have is the restricter of intellect and intelligence, so we have a restricted two dimensional time perspective, and tend to think two dimensionally about the universe. As we become more enlightened, we have this implant "tuned up" or even replaced to let us "see" more clearly.

Examples of what the implants affect are: spiritual balance (how restricted is your enlightenment?), intelligence (as mentioned), your tolerance and temper, your wisdom, your talents and your inner peace. Your birth imprint may set you up as a hot-headed heavy-set sick person. but the implants can change that 180 degrees as you go through your karma. It is critically important to remember the premise for all this. You choose it before you arrive in the infinite wisdom and love as the piece of God that you represent when you are not in "lesson."

The biggest use for the implant by the universe is to RELEASE you from your karma. When you have successfully moved through a period in your life that satisfies your karmic lesson, you are rewarded with an implant that **releases** the part of your birth imprint that set up the original lesson. When compared to the earlier hose analogy, it is like turning off specific spigots when the lawn is watered enough in certain areas. The water pressure is still there, but you are finished with it in those areas, so you void it by turning the spigots off, and releasing the need for the pressure.

Calling for the **neutral implant** is like asking the Universe for a **RELEASE**, and is the new privilege as reported by Kryon. In the new energy of our planet the Universe is offering you special master guides, that through your intent will come in and give you a set of super neutralizing attributes that almost void out all the life properties that your birth imprint gave you. You can now do away with most spiritual birth traits - throw away all your karmic lessons, gain more enlightenment (and with it get more wisdom, tolerance and peace), become balanced and healthy and *prepare yourself to work* with healing the planet. No wonder some are calling the implant "The Release!" The mechanics of this release is the message of this book, by way of the special loving writings of the master Kryon.

Interwoven in all of this is the fact that in taking the karmic release, you help in the transmutation of negative to positive for the planet in a way that was not possible a short while ago.

Dear friend, whoever you are, I hope this has helped you. You and I have a common bond connected by the unbreakable thread of the love energy that is now gaining strength. We are all part of the same family of humans, trying our best to live on this planet in peace. Pass this book to a friend when you are finished, the most important thing is that this message gets out to all those who are ready.

Offered in love,   Lee Carroll
                        (The writer)

The Kryon Attack!

In February 1996, an organization based out of Tucson, Arizona, launched an all-out attack on the Kryon work. The woman who leads the group proclaimed that Kryon was the "great cosmic evil of the century." She sent out thousands of newsletters to light workers and bookstores announcing that the neutral implant was a Kryon trick (even though astrological, spiritual, and religious books have talked about the neutral implant, or *Bridge of Swords*, for centuries). Plus, many of those close to the Kryon work received personal letters or phone calls at their homes, and there was an attack in the Kryon forum on *America Online*.

This barrage of negativity concerned and frightened many. Fear does that, and her message was fear based. I had numerous letters asking about this, and we had several *Kryon Quarterly* magazine subscribers in Arizona cancel their subscriptions. Needless to say, this attack stirred the pot!

A national metaphysical backlash resulted, with many New Age magazines publishing articles taking the woman to task for her tactics, and for not printing factual information. Some of the articles even gave examples of how her writings, taken only from this first Kryon book (not considering information from the 6 others), had been paraphrased, yet quoted to achieve her own purposes. Phrases were lifted from areas more than ten pages apart, then rearranged into a single sentence to appear to support her allegations.

I was personally saddened by the attack, but even more disheartened to see positive, enthusiastic light workers distracted over the events, and disillusioned that such a thing would happen within the spiritual community.

I ultimately went to Tucson to investigate the woman's motives. I learned that this was not the first time she had publicly blasted another well-known light worker. In fact, in the mid-1980s she assailed a very old, feeble oracle in New York in a similar manner, and ended up causing a coup and dethroning the oracle, taking with her a large part of the lucrative following (and mailing list). So unfortunately, much of this appears to be about power and money, old-energy concepts that we can now easily transmute with love.

Even though her tactics have been unmasked, her attack continues into areas of the world such as Europe and Asia where there are fresh light workers to frighten.

To those who were faced with inner questions as a result of these attacks, I applaud you for using your tools of discernment. To those who wrote letters of support and encouragement, I thank you for your love and prayers.

As a Kryon reader, I thought you should know the rest of the story.

Lee Carroll

Kryon at The United Nations!

In November 1995, November 1996, and again in November 1998, Kryon spoke at the S.E.A.T. (Society for Enlightenment and Transformation) at the United Nations in New York City. By invitation Jan and Lee brought a time of lecture, toning, meditation and channeling to an elite group of UN delegates and guests.

Kryon Book 6, *Partnering With God* carried the first two entire transcripts of what Kryon had to say ... some of which has now been validated by the scientific community. All three of these transcripts are on the Kryon web site [www.kryon.com].

Our sincere thanks to Mohamad Ramadan in 1995, Cristine Arismendy in 1996, and Jennifer Borchers in 1998 who were presidents of that bright spot at the United Nations, for the invitation and for their work to enlighten our planet.

Appendix A
Questions about the Implant/Release

I t's time to address a select few questions from the reader's of this book. During the first year of the Kryon book pre-publication (the non-paperback teacher's edition), the letters came steadily from all over the northern hemisphere asking questions and re-questing more information. The following are selected questions written to Kryon by some of those readers about self-discovery, and the implant/release. I have not used any reader's name, city, country or even initials since I have kept some of the personal remarks by Kryon so that you can relate to these compassionate answers. Therefore I feel I have maintained the integrity of the confidential communication. These questions (as well as many more) are also included in Kryon Book II "*Don't Think Like a Human,*" but are included here as well since they are so important to the subject of the implant/release. This section has been included starting with the 2nd reprint of this book in 1994.

Question: I asked for the neutral implant, karmic release but don't know if my request was accepted yet or not. I have begun to experience more vivid dreams which is very unusual for me and I experienced depression of a more severe degree and length than normally I have at this phase in my life. It is possible that these are related to the power of suggestion or that my guides have left in readiness for the master guides?

Answer: Dear one, the very moment you read that you could ask for the implant, and committed to do it verbally, began the changes in your life. Remember that Spirit knows you and is not in your linear time frame. This means that we were in preparation for what you wanted long before you asked for it. Your new guides had arrived and were standing by at the very time you expressed the intent.

Intent is honored by the universe as much as a verbal promise in your culture and therefore it is the way of things that your request was immediately granted. Do not ever try to "analyze away" in a mental way what your intuition tells you is happening. This will not serve you. You should look forward to more enlightenment and a wiser feeling about those around you in the near future.

Question: I find myself afraid to go through the challenging things that the book said I might. I want the implant/release, but I don't want darkness or depression. I am also afraid that I might lose my husband as well... and I don't want to. Am I confused?

Answer: If more humans could express their fear verbally and as you have done in transcription, they would have a far better understanding of their karmic attributes. Let me answer your question in general then specifically: it is common for the humanness in one to fear the astral, and this in itself is a phantom; something that is not as it appears. Do not fear the implant. Ever! The implant is the first step toward greeting the higher self; that part of you that has been suspended, waiting to come in to finally greet you and become one. You may have confused the implant and some of the transitions of its implementation with some Earth ritual that asks you to sacrifice something in order to have something. Nothing like this is occurring with the implant. Instead, you are being prepared and cleaned so that you can accept mature wisdom, and inner peace, and of course lack of fear. Don't mistake this process for any kind of sacrifice! When you clean your body before you put on new clothes, does it hurt? There is no punishment here. Also know this: when you ask for the implant, you are asking for your contract to be complete. This is your perfect scenario and there could be no better place for you than fulfilling it. The universe will not give you something negative when it gives you the tool to complete your contract!

Dear one, you are so afraid of being abandoned, it shouts from your very soul. This indeed is your karmic attribute, and is the one that will be voided. You fear being alone without the guides and you fear the loss of your partner. Understand that the implant will begin to clear this fear. Specifically in your case when you no longer exhibit fear of abandonment, your partner will know something is different, and you will become a far more stable partner for him. Look forward to a far better relationship when you are balanced, and finally have this karma of fear removed from you. Only those whose partners and mates were specifically there to play out karma will leave, and yours is not one of these. Do not fear the implant. One new guide is already in place due to your expression of intent, and you will have an easy time with the others as well. We love you without measure... just as your human parents were supposed to have done... and did not. Spirit will not forsake you.

Question: I know that I want to call for the guide change and karmic release but at this moment I wished that I lived nearer to you so that we could have a counselling session! My fear is that if I take the implant/release, I may cause pain to my family. I have two children aged 15 and 10. I know I have karmic links with them, and I am in a dilemma, for I don't want to lose them.

Answer: I sat at the feet of a lovely human mother last week in private channel who was admonished to "place her children on the altar of Spirit, and have peace." This is a direct reference to the very old story of Abraham and Isaac where Spirit wanted to give a very strong message for history that in order to save your children, you must be willing to sacrifice them to God.

The message is clear for you as well: These precious entities will be with you for their time of raising, and they will not be removed from you if you are willing to raise them under the umbrella of Spirit. In fact, dear one in your case, your change (due to the neutral implant) will affect your children in a positive manner, which is directly in your contract. Instead of losing them, you will give them a great gift that would not be given otherwise. This is the tremendous beauty of how Spirit works. Be willing, and Spirit honors intent (to the letter).

The neutral implant changes YOU, which in turn affects others around you and makes you a co-creator with Spirit for the things in your life that you need. The thing that changes the most is FEAR. Fear of things that otherwise would send you into spirals of imbalance suddenly retreat from you, and you stand there wondering what happened. You get balance in the process; something your children will see, enjoy and try to emulate for the rest of their lives. Long after you are gone they will remember how their mother reacted and dealt with events and people, and these things will affect them. This is your contract with the young ones. This is why you received the book. Please be peaceful with this and let Spirit know (verbally) that you recognize the contract with the children, as you ask to proceed to the next level. Can you see the love that goes into all this?

Question: I don't want to become a person without emotion. Will the karmic release make me passive? If I no longer react to the drama of neutralized karma... what is there? Will I laugh?

Answer: That part of you which is human and laughs – and is joyful – and loves – is one of the only parts of Spirit that passes to you unchanged when you arrive on your planet. Believe me, your question alone is very humorous indeed!

When you receive the real peace of Spirit, you receive an empty emotional agenda. Understand what this means: this does not mean that the emotions are no longer there... it only means that you are now free to use them without wasting them on karma! No more worry or fear or anger. Now you can turn the former drama of karmic interaction to the far more pleasing and positive attributes of celebration, joy, love and yes, even humor. Especially humor. Are you laughing?

Question: I have children 3 & 6. I am afraid to petition for the karmic release, since I am afraid of losing them. I am also uncertain what will happen between my husband and me. Although he is not a spiritual man, he is a good father and husband. I don't want to lose him either. What should I do?

Answer: Immediately give intent for the spiritual karmic implant/release. For you and all humans know this: this release is your reward. There is absolutely no sacrifice or suffering involved in this process. Those who leave your life will be the appropriate ones; the ones you are finished with; the ones who are here to complete karma with you. The transition period is difficult for some, especially for those who are deeply involved in karmic attributes. Those like you, who are poised and ready for change, and who realize basic truth when it is presented, will not have a great deal of trouble exchanging guides.

Let me speak of your children. This is important for you to see. The children and you chose each other carefully before you came in. They are yours for the duration of the rearing as in the case with all mothers. No mother need ever worry about losing children because of the implant. This is not universally appropriate. Even if the children test your limits of temperament and tolerance, it is appropriate; for the implant will adjust to help with this. What happens after they are grown is another story, for then they will have the responsibility to Spirit and karma just as you do now, and will deal with you then in relation to that. The universe loves the children as much as you do, and needs you there to take care of them until they get their own enlightenment, perhaps with your help. Look into their eyes sometime and try to "recognize" them. Ask for information from Spirit on this. It is often given in dreams and may be amusing, ironic and useful to know who they "really" are.

As for your husband, his spirituality has nothing whatsoever to do with what will happen to you if you call for the gift of the karmic release. He is loved every bit as much as any human in lesson and has his own path and process. Your involvement with him and the resulting children are indeed part of your karma. But what happens after the release does not have to be negative. The messages in the first part of this book are warnings of what could potentially happen, so that those with the heaviest karma would be ready. If he is tolerant of your process and lets you alone in your personal quest, then it shows you the karma between the two of you is not of the kind that would remove him. Your partnership is very appropriate based on what happened in past lives, and is not a heavy attribute. Taking the implant/release will change you, but he may enjoy the change and comment on it, making the partnership better. There is never a need for any balanced human to evangelize the new power, and no human will ever call for the release in order to make anyone around them "wrong" because the other didn't ask for it. The resulting wisdom and balance involved in the karmic release precludes this.

Would you like to be on the Kryon mailing list?

This list is used to inform interested people of Kryon workshops coming to their areas, new Kryon releases, and Kryon news in general. We don't sell or distribute our lists to anyone.

If you would like to be included, please simply drop a post card to us that says "LIST," and include your clearly printed name and address.

The Kryon Writings

1155 Camino Del Mar – #422
Del Mar, California 92014

Timely. Informative. Provocative.

Kryon

QUARTERLY

MAGAZINE

The *Kryon Quarterly* magazine brings you timely information about our transformation into the New Age with four information-packed issues per year. It's filled with the latest Kryon channels and parables, science and medical news, reader questions, astrology, inner child features, how-to information about working with your New Age tools, upcoming seminar schedules and much more. Stay tuned to the latest news about these changing times by subscribing to the *Kryon Quarterly*. Just $24 for four issues; $40 for eight issues. (*Australia and New Zealand - see below**)

Kryon Audio products

Kryon Live Channeled Audio Tapes

▶ **Ascension in The New Age** - ISBN 1-888053-01-1 • $10.00
Carlsbad, California - "Kryon describes what ascension really is in the new age.
It might surprise you!"

▶ **Nine Ways to Raise the Planet's Vibration** - ISBN 1-888053-00-3 • $10.00
Seattle, Washington - "Raising the planet's vibration is the goal of humanity!
Find out what Kryon has to say about it."

▶ **Gifts and Tools of The New Age** - ISBN 1-888053-03-8 • $10.00
Casper, Wyoming - "A very powerful channel. Better put on your sword, shield
and armor for this one."

▶ **Co-Creation in The New Age** - ISBN 1-888053-04-6 • $10.00
Portland, Oregon - "Tired of being swept around in life? Find out about
co-creating your own reality. It is our right in this new age!"

▶ **Seven Responsibilities of The New Age** - ISBN 1-888053-02-X • $10.00
Indianapolis, Indiana - "Responsibility? For what? Find out what Spirit tells us
we are now in charge of...and what to do with it."

Music and Meditation

▶ **Crystal Singer Music Meditation Tape -** ISBN 0-96363-4-1-5 • $10.00
Enjoy two soaring 17 minute musical meditations featuring the beautiful singing
voice of Jan Tober.

▶ **Guided Meditations Tape -** ISBN 1-388053-05-4 • $10.00
Jan presents two guided meditations similar to those delivered at each Kryon seminar
throughout the United States and Canada, with beautiful Celtic harp accompaniment
by Mark Geisler.   Side One: "Finding Your Sweet Spot"   Side Two: "Divine Love"

▶ **Color & Sound Meditation CD -** ISBN 1-888053-06-2 • $15.00
A complete color/sound workshop — an exercise to balance and harmonize the Chakras.
Jan guides us through the seven Chakra system using the enhancement of the ancient
Tibetan signing bowls.   Side One: 30-min meditation   Side Two: 12-min meditation

Kryon Books On Tape

Published by **AUDIO LITERATURE** *Read by Lee Carroll*

▶ **The End Times -** ISBN 1-57453-168-9
▶ **Don't Think Like A Human -** ISBN 1-57453-169-7
▶ **Alchemy Of The Human Spirit -** ISBN 1-57453-170-0
Each audio book contains two cassettes, 3 hours, abridged - $17.95

▶ **"The Parables of Kryon" -** *Read by Lee Carroll*
Published by **Hay House** *and scored with music!* ISBN 1-56170-454-7 - $16.95

▶ **"The Journey Home"** *Unabridged !* - *Read by Lee Carroll*
Published by **Hay House** - *a six tape set!* ISBN 1-56170-453-9 - $30.00
(seven hour listening experience)

Books and tapes can be purchased in retail stores, or by phone
~ Credit cards welcome ~ 1-800-352-6657

products

Kryon Book One: "The End Times"

Published by **The Kryon Writings, Inc.** ISBN 0-9636304-2-3 (White Cover) $12.00

"This read is a can't-put-it-down-til-the-last-page experience"
New Age Retailer - Washington

Kryon Book Two: "Don't Think Like A Human"

Published by **The Kryon Writings, Inc.** ISBN 0-9636304-0-7 (Blue Cover) $12.00

"The simple manner in which the material is presented
makes this a highly accessible work for newcomers to Metaphysics"
Connecting Link - Magazine, Michigan

Kryon Book Three: "The Alchemy of The Human Spirit"

Published by **The Kryon Writings, Inc.** ISBN 0-9636304-8-2 (Fuchsia Cover) $14.00

"The words of Kryon are loving, peaceful and reassuring.
There is a lot of great news"
The Light Connection - San Diego

Kryon Book Four: "The Parables of Kryon"

Published by **Hay House** ISBN 1-56170-364-8 $17.00 (hard cover - with illustrations)

"For anyone who is ready for the next evolutionary step, this information from
Kryon is invaluable. It is both self-healing and planetary healing...Kryon really
lets us know that all is well and we have work to do"
Louise L. Hay - Best-Selling Author

Kryon Book Five: "The Journey Home"

Published by **Hay House** ISBN 1-56170-399-0 $14.95 (hard cover - with illustrations))
ISBN 1-56170-552-7 $11.95 (soft cover)

"Lee Carroll has given us a well written book that flows like a mighty river. And that
river takes us to places like truth, hope, destiny, awareness, and home!"

Richard Fuller - Metaphysical Reviews

Kryon Book Six: "Partnering with God"

Published by **The Kryon Writings, Inc.** ISBN 1-888053-10-0 (Green Cover) $14.00

"If you liked the original Kryon series, you are going to love this book! - Probably the
most practical Kryon book yet. All 400 pages are packed with the love of God for
humanity...a stirring read."
New Age Retailer - Washington

Books and tapes can be purchased in retail stores, or by phone
~ Credit cards welcome ~
1-800-352-6657

Index

For those using the Kryon material for study, the following index is a guide to find the words and/or subjects as listed below.

Index (continued)

About the writer and his work:

Lee Carroll is a California businessman who was neither an active Metaphysician or an author. His degrees are in Business Administration and Economics from California Western University, Point Loma, California. His technical line of work is sound recording for broadcast, and he holds many Clio and IBA awards for his work. At 48, he began what is obviously his real purpose in this life, the translations of Kryon... and you are holding the first book published in 1993 (twice revised).

This book is just one of eight books by Lee (as of 5/99). There are also 13 audio tapes of books on tape, music, meditations and live channeling. In 1996 the *Kryon Quarterly Magazine* was launched, featuring recent channelings, news about earth changes, questions and answers for Kryon, and comments from readers. At this writing the KQ now has over 3,400 subscribers in over 12 countries. Kryon also has His own America On-Line area, and two very active linked internet sites (see page 112/113 - www.kryonqtly.com).

Lee's practical bottom-line approach to almost everything brings out the kind of translations that are easy to read, and yet make sense of even the most cryptic concepts received during channel. His admonishments by the magnetic master are (1) Don't build a church (2) Don't elicit followers (3) Don't make the work evangelistic (3) Do not build a large organization around the work (4) Don't channel on live broadcast. The scientific validations of Kryon's information began appearing in mainstream periodicals about 8 months after this book was published, and are presented in most of the other Kryon books, and regularly in the Quarterly Magazine.

Kryon is now channeling live around the United States, Europe, and Asia, and has presented at the S.E.A.T. in New York at the United Nations three times. The books are being translated in many foreign languages including French, German, Danish, Hebrew, Spanish and Chinese. For a daily updated schedule of Kryon events, please see the Kryon web site (www.kryonqtly.com).

The Kryon Writings

1155 Camino Del Mar – #422
Del Mar, California 92014